No Place for a Child

Child___ __ UK immigration detention:
Impa__ ___ __ __ _d safeguards

Heav_n Cr___ __ _d Tr__ _ Lester

Save the Children

Save the Children fights for children in the UK and around the world who suffer from poverty, disease, injustice and violence. We work with them to find lifelong answers to the problems they face.

Save the Children UK is a member of the International Save the Children Alliance, the world's leading independent children's rights organisation, with members in 27 countries and operational programmes in more than 100.

Published by
Save the Children
1 St John's Lane
London EC1M 4AR
UK

Tel +44 (0)20 7012 6400

First published 2005

© The Save the Children Fund 2005

Registered Company No. 178159

ISBN 1 84187 103 6

Executive summary compiled by Elli Free

Typeset by Avon DataSet Ltd, Bidford on Avon, Warwickshire
Printed by Page Bros (Norwich) Ltd, UK

Contents

Abbreviations

AAP	Appearance Assistance Programme
AVID	Association of Visitors to Immigration Detainees
BID	Bail for Immigration Detainees
CIO	Chief Immigration Officer
CLR	Controlled Legal Representation
DEPMU	Detention Escort and Population Management Unit, IND
DfES	Department for Education and Skills
DOF	Detention Overspill Facility (Oakington)
DSPU	Detention Services Policy Unit, IND
ECHR	European Convention on Human Rights
ECRE	European Council on Refugees and Exiles
ELR	Exceptional Leave to Remain (now Humanitarian Protection or Discretionary Leave)
HMIE	Her Majesty's Inspectorate of Education
HMIP	Her Majesty's Inspectorate of Prisons
HRA	Human Rights Act
HREOC (Australia)	Human Rights and Equal Opportunity Commission
IAA	Immigration Appellate Authority
IAS	Immigration Advisory Service
IAT	Immigration Appeal Tribunal
ILPA	Immigration Law Practitioners' Association
IND	Immigration and Nationality Directorate, Home Office
IOM	International Organisation for Migration
IRSS	Immigration Research and Statistics Service, Home Office
MODCU	Management of Detained Cases Unit, IND
NRUC	National Register of Unaccompanied Asylum Seeking Children
NASS	National Asylum Support Service
NSA	Non-Suspensive Appeals
NSPCC	National Society for the Prevention of Cruelty to Children
OEM	Operational Enforcement Manual
RCC	Refugee Children's Consortium
RLC	Refugee Legal Centre
TA	Temporary Admission
UNCRC	UN Convention on the Rights of the Child
UNHCR	United Nations High Commission(er) for Refugees
VAR(R)P	Voluntary Assisted Returns (and Reintegration) Programme

Acknowledgments

We would like to thank all of those at Save the Children who supported and advised us from the conception of this research to its conclusion. Particular thanks are due to Miranda Kaunang in the England Programme and to Richard Morran for assistance with our visit to Glasgow and Dungavel. Thanks are also due to Amanda McDowell and Laura Brownlees.

The research undertaken for this project was made possible by the considerable support, input and interest shown by a large number of people working across the voluntary sector and within government. We would like to thank all the stakeholders and practitioners who agreed to be interviewed by us and who are named individually at the end of this report, as well as all those who participated in the roundtable discussion and provided ideas and feedback on our emerging research findings. Particular thanks are due to Sarah Cutler at Bail for Immigration Detainees for providing us with case study information and for her input into all aspects of this project, to Richard Lumley at the Refugee Council for his role as part of the project Advisory Group, Sally Tarshish and Helen Ireland at Association of Visitors to immigration Detainees who provided us with ideas and information, and Susan Rowlands at Immigration Law Practitioners' Association and Helen Johnson at the Refugee Council Children's Panel for commenting on earlier drafts.

We are indebted to BID for helping us to identify and access case study respondents, Maureen McCamley and Taiwo Babatunde at the Refugee Council Children's Panel, and Sister Bernadette at Asylum Welcome for putting us in touch with potential interviewees. Our thanks also to the Children's Legal Centre, Immigration Advisory Service, Immigration Law Practitioners' Association, Refugee Legal Centre and Refugee Legal Group for helping us to collect case study information.

Last but by no means least, a very special acknowledgement is due to those families and children who agreed to speak to us about their experiences of being detained in the UK. Although we are not able to identify them individually, we are extremely grateful for the information they gave us and for their willingness to talk to us about what were clearly very difficult times in their lives.

Dr Heaven Crawley
Trine Lester
AMRE Consulting

Foreword

Children who come to the UK as refugees may be doing so because of fear of persecution, human rights violation or armed conflict in their own country. They may be the victims of trafficking for sexual, labour or other exploitation, or they may have travelled to escape conditions of serious deprivation. They may have come with their families, or they may be alone.

Whatever the reasons, refugee children come to the UK to seek protection. Yet on arrival they enter a legal process that is complex and confusing, and they may find themselves detained for any amount of time and at any stage as part of that process, without having committed an offence. Little is known about the reasons for their detention, the length of time they are detained, or the impact this has on their well-being as there is limited official information on this subject. What is known is that the detention of children for the purposes of immigration control runs contrary to a range of international human rights standards relating to the treatment of children.

This research set out to explore the reasons why children are increasingly being detained and the impact it has on their lives, and to analyse and recommend workable alternatives to the detention of children for immigration reasons.

The findings presented in this report are disturbing. They illustrate clearly that detention is no place for a child: it can be hugely detrimental to their well-being and can have long-lasting negative effects. Crucially, the findings also show that a substantial gap exists between the stated policy objectives of detaining children as a 'last resort', and the reality of current practice which sees children detained unnecessarily. Finally, the report highlights failures in government policy and practice to safeguard and protect these vulnerable children.

The report presents a number of viable alternatives to detention, some of which have been seen to work successfully in practice. In the light of the research findings, Save the Children is calling on the Government to consider seriously the alternatives, and to adopt them as soon as possible to make the detention of refugee children a thing of the past.

Mike Aaronson
Director General
Save the Children UK

Executive summary

"I spent eight months and 24 days [in detention] . . . it was the hardest time of my life. It's hell. Prison is better than detention . . . In prison, you have rights, not veiled rights. In detention, you have no rights . . ."

(Jacques, aged 17)

About this study

This report examines the experience of children who are detained for the purpose of immigration control. It explores the impacts of detention on children, the alternatives to detention and the safeguards that are necessary to prevent detention becoming prolonged and to ensure that children's rights are upheld and that they are treated lawfully.

This report is based on:
- 32 case studies of children who have been detained in the UK either with their parents or as separated children whose age is disputed
- observational visits to two detention centres
- interviews with more than 40 government officials, policy makers, practitioners and stakeholders
- an extensive literature review.

The policy context

The detention of children for the purpose of immigration control runs contrary to a range of international standards relating to the treatment of children and prisoners set by the UN Convention on the Rights of the Child (UNCRC) and the United Nations High Commissioner for Refugees (UNHCR). In recognition of the particular vulnerabilities of children, international law and policy places the needs of children above the requirements of immigration control. The UK Government, however, entered a Reservation to the UNCRC, which effectively allows children who are subject to immigration control to be excluded from its provision. Save the Children Alliance and UNHCR believe that children should never be detained for immigration reasons alone.

There is a growing use of detention centres to meet the objectives of UK asylum and immigration policy, including fast track processing of asylum applications and an increased emphasis on removals. These recent policy changes and failures in practice relating to age-disputed asylum-seekers mean that both children in families and those who have become separated from their parents or other carers are increasingly liable to be detained. This is in spite of the fact that Her Majesty's Chief Inspector of Prisons has recommended that the detention of children should be an exceptional measure and for very short periods – no more than a matter of days.

The findings

1. Numbers and length of time in detention
The report estimates that around 2,000 children are detained with their families every year for the purpose of immigration control. There is no government data on the number of cases in which the age of an asylum applicant is disputed and detained.[1] Current UK policy and practice means that children can and do remain in detention for lengthy periods. In the cases that were studied, the length of detention varied considerably from 7 days to 268 days. Half (16) of all cases looked at were detained for more than 28 days.

2. Separated children and disputes over age
There is evidence that the number of age-disputed asylum-seekers has increased and that a significant proportion of those who are detained are found to be children who are separated from their parents/carers. The report raises significant concerns about the detention of these children, including mental health

problems, lack of access to education, and child protection concerns. The research found that social service age assessments are not routinely undertaken and even when they are the Home Office does not always take them into account, contrary to stated policy.

3. The impacts of detention

Children in immigration detention are triply at risk as children, detainees and asylum-seekers.

- **Mental health** The greatest negative impacts are on mental health. Children can suffer from a deterioration in mental health, including depression, changes in behaviour and confusion. Mental health problems in detention can have long-term consequences.
- **Physical health** Parents were particularly concerned about their children's refusal to eat and eating an unbalanced diet. Not being able to sleep and persistent coughs (most evident in those in detention for over 100 days) were also common problems. Detainees also lacked confidence in the medical staff.
- **Education** The disruption to mainstream schooling during and after detention and the learning environment in detention has a damaging impact on children's education. The research also found that the general and sometimes overwhelming impacts of detention on mental health undermined the ability and willingness of many children to learn.

4. The decision to detain

Children are currently detained in the UK as part of fast track procedures for asylum determination. Processes for ensuring that there are no obstacles to removal and that the welfare of children is taken into account in the decision to detain are not always effective. This increases the risk that children will be detained unnecessarily or without any imminent prospect for their removal. There is rarely any evidence to suggest that they would not comply with the conditions of Temporary Admission if they were not detained.

5. Detention review procedures

The report raises significant concerns about the effectiveness of existing review procedures for ensuring that the detention of children is not prolonged. There is evidence that the review process is dominated by immigration-related issues and that the welfare of children is not a key consideration in the continuing decision to detain.

6. Lack of legal advice

There is a lack of access to quality legal advice and representation in detention which undermines the effectiveness of bail as a mechanism for safeguarding children who are detained. Lack of good legal advice for age-disputed children means that they are often unable to access formal age assessment procedures.

7. Transfers between detention centres

Unexpected, unexplained and sometimes frequent transfers between detention centres are common. Transfers exacerbated the negative impacts of detention on children causing distress, disorientation and loss of contact between detainees and their families, friends and legal representatives.

8. Child protection concerns

Current safeguards are inadequate for ensuring that children are not subject to abuse while in detention or removed from the UK with their abuser. The risks to age-disputed children who are detained with adults in communal sleeping facilities are not recognised.

Conclusions and recommendations

The evidence in this report suggests the need for an entirely different approach towards children who are subject to immigration control, one that places their needs and interests as children at the centre of decision-making. To deliver this approach the report explores a range of alternatives to detention in line with international standards and guidelines which state that asylum-seeking children should not be detained. The report recommends that the UK Government should review its practice and in particular:

1. Treat asylum-seeking children as children first and foremost. If the Government is serious about protecting and safeguarding the interests of children in the UK, then asylum-seeking and other migrant children must be treated as children first and foremost. The reservation to the UNCRC should be withdrawn and their interests and needs represented by the Commissioners for Children and Young People in England, Wales, Scotland and Northern Ireland.

2. Do not detain children for the purpose of immigration control because of the negative physical, mental and educational consequences of detention. This includes the use of detention for children as part of fast track or accelerated procedures for asylum determination. Alternatives should be developed for ensuring compliance where this is considered necessary.

3. Improve age assessment procedures. Formal age assessments should be undertaken by social services or an independent age assessment panel *prior* to a decision to detain. No individual whose age is disputed should be detained unless and until such an assessment is undertaken.

4. Reporting. Existing reporting mechanisms should be made more user-friendly and should be flexible to the needs of families with children. The Home Office should cover the cost of all reporting requirements. Where reporting arrangements break down, efforts should be made to re-establish contact before any decisions are made to detain.

5. Develop alternatives to detention. The Home Office should pilot a system of incentivised compliance. This system should be based on the Appearance Assistance Program (AAP) in the United States and a similar system in Sweden. These approaches provide a combination of freedom from detention, a graduated scale of supervision, individualised needs and risk assessment and support, primarily through provision of information and legal advice and representation from the beginning of the asylum determination process.

6. Improve voluntary returns. Information about the opportunities for returning voluntarily to the country of origin needs to be made more widely available. Return under these circumstances must be truly voluntary in order for it to be effective and durable.

Recommendations to help children in detention now

- A statutory **time limit** of a maximum of seven days should be placed on the detention of children.
- Further action should be taken to monitor and significantly **reduce the transfer of children** between detention facilities.
- **Legal advice** and representation should be available to all detainees. Access to bail should be actively facilitated and properly funded.
- **Detailed statistics** on the immigration detention of children and age-disputed cases should be published on a regular basis.
- All staff working in removal centres should undergo enhanced Criminal Records Bureau checks, and families with children about whom there are **child protection concerns** should not be removed from the UK unless and until these issues are resolved.
- **Assessments and review processes** need to improve, including:
  - Case-by-case assessments should be carried out to establish whether it would be better for a child to be detained with his or her family, or separated, and parents and their children should be part of this decision-making process.
  - No families with children should be detained without a full review of their case by an enforcement officer. A pastoral visit by the Home Office should always be undertaken prior to a decision to detain.
  - In the absence of a statutory time limit to detention, there should be an independent process for reviewing all cases where children are detained.
  - Welfare assessments panels at seven and 21 days should be introduced for all children in detention.

Note

1 Assessing the exact numbers of children detained in the UK and the length of time for which they are detained is impossible because of significant gaps in the evidence base.

1 Introduction

At first I could manage it. But I couldn't sleep and I deteriorated. In detention you never see immigration. You are in limbo . . . you never know if they are coming to get you. Every time they gave me removal directions, I would wait for them to come and get me, but they didn't. I didn't know why I was there.

Jacques was 16 years old when he arrived in the UK and applied for asylum. The Home Office disputed his age, his application was refused, and he was subsequently detained. His detention lasted nearly nine months before he was released.

The detention of children like Jacques is of increasing concern because a substantial body of evidence shows that detention has serious negative impacts on their physical and mental health. Save the Children has a long-standing interest in the experiences of asylum-seeking and refugee children in the UK. Together with a wide range of international and UK-based organisations, it believes that no child should be detained for the purpose of immigration control.

The UK Government states that it detains children only as a matter of last resort, in cases where there is no other alternative for ensuring compliance with immigration procedures. Save the Children commissioned this report in response to a call from the former Home Secretary, David Blunkett MP, for critics of the immigration detention of children to propose alternative solutions.[2] Believing that immigration detention is no place for a child, Save the Children wanted to explore the Government's justification of detention as a last resort, to highlight safeguards for children who are in detention at present and to identify viable alternatives that would enable the Government to make the immigration detention of children a thing of the past.

1.1 Research aims and focus

In recent years a wide range of organisations and individuals have expressed concerns about the detention of children in the UK for the purpose of immigration control. These concerns have largely focused on the detention of children with their families at the Dungavel Removal Centre in Lanarkshire, Scotland. This facility, which contains a unit specifically designed for families who are being detained pending their removal from the UK, was the focus of an inspection by Her Majesty's Inspectorate of Prisons (HMIP) in October 2002. The inspection report recommended that the detention of children should be an exceptional measure and for very short periods – no more than a matter of days (HMIP 2002: 7):

The key principle here is not the precise number of days . . . It is that the welfare and development of children is likely to be compromised by detention, however humane the provisions, and that this will increase the longer detention is maintained.

HMIP's concerns about the detention of children were reiterated in its report following an inspection of Oakington Removal Centre (HMIP 2004).

During this period there have also been a number of high-profile cases involving families detained at Dungavel for lengthy periods of time, which have galvanised opposition from local politicians, the voluntary sector, and some sections of the media. For example, Mrs Ay and her four children – now aged between eight and 14 years – spent more than a year in Dungavel before being deported to Germany in August 2003. Ms Konan and her daughter were detained at Harmondsworth and Dungavel Removal Centres for more than six months, despite evidence that the health of both mother and child were being damaged. Ms Konan was finally granted bail and was subsequently recognised as a Convention refugee. In January 2004 a High Court judge ruled that all but the initial two-week period of her detention was unlawful.[3] As a result of these and other cases involving children who have been detained for exceptionally lengthy periods, the issue of children in immigration detention has been debated on a number of separate occasions in both the House of Commons and House of Lords.

The aim of our research is to examine the experiences of asylum-seeking children (defined in international and UK law as being under 18 years of age) who are detained in the UK in order to identify a) the use of detention and its impacts; and b) the alternative mechanisms available to the Immigration and Nationality Directorate (IND) for maintaining contact with families and ensuring compliance with immigration controls. We are interested in finding out whether the detention of children in the UK is, as the Home Office argues, a necessary and proportionate response because, if they were not detained, families would simply abscond or otherwise fail to comply with directions for their removal from the UK. We are also interested in knowing whether once a decision to detain has been made, the safeguards put in place to prevent the prolonged detention of children are accessible and effective.

We have focused our analysis on those seeking asylum in the UK, although the use of detention to enforce immigration control is not limited to this group. Anyone who has entered the UK illegally or has breached his or her conditions of entry or stay is liable to be detained. This is important because it has implications for the numbers of non-asylum seeking children who are liable to be detained for the purposes of immigration control, particularly given the increase in channels for 'managed migration' into the UK. Many of the issues identified apply equally to other groups of children. Children's immigration status or that of their family does not alter the fact that they are children first and foremost and many of their basic needs and aspirations will be no different from those of other children in the UK. Nonetheless, specific issues arise by virtue of being involved in the asylum system, which have significant implications

both for the decision to detain and for the alternatives that are available to policy-makers.

Finally, it should be noted that although our research considers in some detail the impacts of detention on children, the focus of our analysis and recommendations is on alternatives to the use of detention and on ensuring that there are safeguards for reducing the length of time spent in detention, where such a decision is taken. With the exception of broader child protection and 'duty of care' issues, we do not examine in any detail the levels of provision, for example, in terms of educational and health facilities – available for children within immigration detention settings. Both HMIP and Her Majesty's Inspectorate of Education (HMIE) have already undertaken much of this work in Dungavel and Oakington (HMIP 2002, 2004; HMIE 2003). We have taken their findings into account in writing this report.

1.2 The international context

No child shall be deprived of his or her liberty unlawfully or arbitrarily. The arrest, detention or imprisonment of a child shall be in conformity with the law and shall be used only as a measure of last resort and for the shortest appropriate period of time (United Nations Convention on the Rights of the Child (UNCRC), Article 37 (b))

The detention of children for the purpose of immigration control runs contrary to a range of international standards relating to the treatment of children and prisoners. Central among these is the 1989 UN Convention on the Rights of the Child (UNCRC), Article 37 of which prohibits the arbitrary detention of children and requires that States detaining children put in place measures to ensure that the detention is for the shortest period of time possible.[4] This presumption against the detention of asylum-seeking children is reflected in the UNHCR's policy guidelines and statements of position, including its guidelines on unaccompanied asylum-seeking children (UNHCR 1997), revised guidelines on the detention of asylum-seekers (UNHCR 1999), and ExCom Resolutions (principally No 44).

UNHCR guidance states that ". . . minors who are asylum-seekers should not be detained".[5] It goes on to state that unaccompanied children should be released into the care of family members who already have residency, and where this is not possible, alternative care arrangements should be made with the appropriate childcare authorities. The guidance explicitly states that "all appropriate alternatives to detention should be considered in the case of children accompanying their parents".[6]

Most recently a paper on refugee and asylum-seeking children prepared for the Global Consultations on International Protection reiterates the principle set out in the guidelines quoted above that the detention of asylum-seekers is inherently undesirable, particularly in the case of vulnerable groups including children in families and unaccompanied minors (UNHCR 2002).

1.2.1 UK Reservation to the UNCRC

Recognising the particular vulnerabilities of children, international law and policy places the needs of children above the requirements of immigration control.[7] The UK has, however, entered a Reservation to the UNCRC, which states that:

> The United Kingdom reserves the right to apply such legislation, in so far as it relates to the entry into, stay in and departure from the United Kingdom on those who do not have the right under the law of the United Kingdom to enter and remain in the United Kingdom, and to the acquisition and possession of citizenship, as it may deem necessary from time to time.

The Reservation effectively allows the Government to exclude children who are subject to immigration control from its provisions.[8] In its initial report to the UN Committee on the Rights of the Child,[9] and in subsequent discussions with Committee members, the Government argued that while the Reservation does not detract from its duties towards refugee children under Article 22,[10] it is necessary in order to maintain the integrity of UK immigration control.

The UK's Reservation to the UNCRC has been widely criticised. The UN Committee on Human Rights has stated that a reservation to an obligation to apply rights on a non-discriminatory basis is inadmissible because it undermines the *universality* of the rights of children and the overall purpose of the Convention itself (Blake and Drew 2001; Baldaccini, 2004). The UN Committee on the Rights of the Child has characterised the broad nature of the Reservation as one of its principal subjects of concern, expressing anxiety about the compatibility of the Reservation with the object and purpose of the CRC itself.[11] The Committee has expressed particular concern that the detention of children claiming asylum, either with their families or on their own, is incompatible with the provisions of the Convention.[12]

There is evidence that although the motivation behind the UK's Reservation was primarily to prevent an obligation to allow the families of separated children into the UK so that they could be reunited, it has been widely interpreted in policy and practice to exclude asylum-seeking and other children subject to immigration control from *all* of the provisions of the UNCRC, including Article 37 on the detention of children. Reflecting this, the Joint Committee on Human Rights (2002) has expressed concern that the Reservation appears to legitimise unequal treatment of asylum-seeking children by both central government and local service providers. To this extent, the Reservation symbolises the relationship between law and policy in the areas of immigration and children more generally. Immigration is one of the few areas of UK law where the child's welfare and best interests are not considered to be the paramount consideration.[13]

1.2.2 European Convention on Human Rights

Finally, whilst not directed specifically at the detention of children, the European Convention on Human Rights (ECHR), incorporated into domestic law through the Human Rights Act (1998), also sets out criteria for the detention of persons subject to immigration control. According to Baldaccini (2004), the only circumstances under which a person subject to immigration control may be detained are in order to prevent unauthorised entry into the country, or when action is being taken with a view to a person's deportation or extradition.

In particular, Article 5 of the ECHR states that failed asylum-seekers cannot be detained without a case-by-case assessment which concludes that if they are not detained they will otherwise fail to comply with removal directions. Although it does not prohibit the detention of asylum-seekers, Article 5 nevertheless subjects this detention to strict conditions and requirements, while at the same time securing concrete, enforceable substantive and procedural rights for detained asylum-seekers (Hughes and Liebaut 1998). Article 5 also states that it is illegal to detain a failed asylum-seeker when removal proceedings have come to a halt. This can be the case if there are legal obstacles to removal, or if factual impediments render return impossible (for example, if the country of origin declines to receive its nationals, or if it is logistically impossible to transport the individual to that country). On this assessment, the use of detention as punishment for non-cooperation or as a measure of deterrence is illegal (Noll 1998).

Although the Home Office has made it clear that it believes current detention policy complies with Article 5 of the ECHR and the Human Rights Act (HRA), the evidence presented in our report suggests that in terms of current practice this is often not the case.

1.3 Detention of children in the UK

1.3.1 Increases in the use of detention

There have been a plethora of changes to asylum and immigration law and policy over recent years, the majority of which have focused on reducing applications for asylum by introducing stricter controls on entry to the UK and on making the asylum process both quicker and firmer. These changes were set out in the 2002 White Paper *Secure Borders, Safe Haven: Integration with Diversity in Modern Britain*,[14] and have resulted in the tightening of external border controls, stricter penalties for those who arrive in the UK without proper documentation, and the introduction of fast track or accelerated procedures for determining applications that are judged to be 'manifestly unfounded' or from countries that are designated as being generally safe.

Detention has been an increasingly important mechanism for delivering the Government's policy objectives in relation to asylum and immigration.[15] The overall increase in the use of detention and the significant increase in capacity of the detention estate have been particularly associated with two aspects of current policy and practice. The first of these is the introduction of the fast track or accelerated procedures for asylum determination. Initially established at Oakington Reception Centre in Cambridgeshire, the aim is to determine cases quickly, generally within seven to ten days.[16] In the Super Fast Track system established at Harmondsworth Removal Centre in March 2003, detention is maintained throughout any appeal process. Currently only male adults are processed at Harmondsworth. There are currently 54 countries listed as being suitable for fast track processing at Oakington. Applicants from 24 of these countries are subject to the Non-Suspensive Appeal (NSA) process and liable for removal from the UK immediately after an initial decision is made on their application for asylum. It seems likely that the use of fast track procedures for NSA and non-NSA cases will increase in the future.

At the same time there has been increased emphasis on removals.[17] This is motivated by a desire by the Government to reduce overall costs, deter future applications and restore the public confidence in the integrity of the asylum system:

We are gradually closing the gap between the number of failed asylum applicants and the number removed. In 1996, the number of removals was equivalent to only 20% of unsuccessful claims. So far this year, that proportion is almost 50%. But I accept we need to do a great deal more . . . Building on our success in reducing applications, we now want a step change in the number of failed applicants who leave this country. By the end of next year, we want the monthly rate of removals to exceed the number of unfounded applications so that we start making in-roads into the backlog.[18]

This is despite the fact that there remain significant concerns about the quality of the decision-making process itself.[19]

1.3.2 Implications for children in families

The increased detention of children must be understood in this broader political and policy context. Until relatively recently, families with children were rarely detained, and then only for a few hours prior to removal. In October 2001, new Immigration Service instructions were issued permitting the detention of families including children for longer periods than immediately prior to removal. This change of policy was reiterated in the 2002 White Paper. As a result of these changes, families with children are now subject to the same policy as single adults. They may be detained at any stage in order to process their claims for asylum quickly, on the grounds that they would otherwise fail to comply with conditions of Temporary Admission or in order to effect removal.

Families with children are not exempted from the fast track procedures and children are now detained with their families in order to enable the Home Office to determine their applications quickly. Neither are they excluded from assumptions that removal will not be achievable without the use of detention. The terms 'non-compliance' and 'abscond' are often used interchangeably to justify a decision to detain where the Home Office believes a family will not comply with Removal Directions (RDs). This judgement may result from a whole range of different circumstances including: when contact between the family and IND has been lost; when additional issues have been raised at the end of the process; when a family expresses a desire to remain in the UK and/or has resisted removal on a previous occasion; or when a family deliberately evades immigration control by taking themselves and their children out of contact with the authorities.

Given that that the Home Office does not know – even in broad outline – what proportion of failed asylum-seekers abscond (Home Affairs Committee 2003), it is not clear whether families would abscond if they were not detained. Evidence presented later in

this report in connection with the Appearance Assistance Programme (AAP) suggests that they would not. What is clear is that the different circumstances under which families are detained can have significant implications for the length of their detention and for the assessment of possible alternatives. It is also worth noting here that recent legislative changes make it more, rather than less, likely that children and young people will be detained in non-immigration detention in the future. For example, section 2 of the Asylum and Immigration Act (2004) makes it an offence for a person not to have a passport or other identity document at a leave or asylum interview, and also makes it an offence for a person not to have such a document in respect of any dependent child with whom he or she claims to be travelling or living.

1.3.3 Detention of age-disputed separated children

Reflecting these policy developments, the detention of children with their families is a major focus of our report. In addition there are widespread and increasing concerns about the detention of children who have become separated from their parents or other carers and who are alone in the UK. It is government policy not to detain unaccompanied or separated children other than in exceptional circumstances (for example, for their own safety while appropriate care arrangements are made), and then for no more than 24 hours. Despite this, there is evidence that asylum applicants whose age is disputed are not being independently age-assessed and are detained as adults.

The failure of decision-makers to give age-disputed asylum-seekers the benefit of the doubt appears to stem largely from a concern within IND that people over the age of 18 sometimes claim to be minors in order to effect release from detention and to gain 'preferential treatment' in the asylum determination process. Concern about the detention of children whose age is disputed has existed for some time (see, for example, Tarshish 1997), but the issue has gained increasing attention over recent months. This is partly because of evidence – arising mostly in the context of the Oakington fast track process – that the number of age-disputed children who are wrongly detained has increased, and partly because issues arising from the unlawful detention of these children have started to reach the courts.

The issue of age assessment goes beyond the scope of this report because it extends to the asylum determination process as a whole and is not limited to issues of detention. Nonetheless, our research raises serious concerns about the lack of consistent processes in place to assess, and respond appropriately to, the needs of individuals whose age is disputed and who are subsequently detained. Moreover, because there is no acknowledgement within current policy and practice that IND may incorrectly assess the age of a child, individuals who are potentially vulnerable, separated children are treated as adults for the purposes of asylum determination. Unlike children who are detained with their parents or carers, no special provision is made for these individuals in terms of health or education. They are held with other adults in settings without any child protection procedures. And none of the safeguards and procedures that have been put in place to prevent the unnecessary or prolonged detention of children apply to this group.

1.3.4 Children Act (2004)

Ironically, separated asylum-seeking children are the very children who are acknowledged in the Government's Green Paper *Every Child Matters* (DfES 2003) to be among the most vulnerable in the UK. However, although this Green Paper was a response to the findings of the inquiry into the death of Victoria Climbié – who was herself a child subject to UK immigration control – it has little else to say about protection for asylum-seeking and migrant children. The resulting Children Act (2004) does not include any provisions dealing with the unsatisfactory situation of separated asylum seeking children and makes no reference to mechanisms for ensuring that other children subject to immigration control are also protected.[20] Indeed the Act explicitly excludes agencies with responsibility for policy and practice in relation to this group of children from its provision. This failure to address the needs of asylum-seeking children was criticised as 'unjustifiable discrimination' by the Joint Committee on Human Rights.[21] The Committee report dismisses the Children's Minister's claim that

extending the duty to safeguard and promote children's welfare to immigration and asylum agencies could conflict with the need to maintain effective immigration control. Rather it views this as proof that the Government sees the welfare of asylum-seeking children as secondary to the overall objective of being – and being seen to be – tough in its use and interpretation of immigration powers.

1.4 How many children are detained and for how long?

1.4.1 Government statistics

As a result of the changes in policy and practice outlined above, children are now detained in three UK removal centres with facilities for families. These are Tinsley House near Gatwick, Oakington in Cambridgeshire and Dungavel House in Lanarkshire.[22] Children whose age is disputed by the Home Office can be detained for any of the same reasons as adults and held in adult immigration removal centres, as well as in prisons and police cell accommodation used for this purpose. Assessing the exact numbers of children detained in the UK and the length of time for which they are detained remains difficult because of significant gaps in the evidence base.

There are several sources of statistical information available in the UK. The Home Office's Immigration Research and Statistics Service (IRSS) have published quarterly detention statistics regarding children since September 2003.[23] These statistics provide a 'snapshot' of the detention estate on a particular day and include information on the detention of families with children. The Home Office also publishes cumulative quarterly statistics for children detained with their families as part of the Oakington NSA process. In addition, unpublished Home Office statistics on the detention of children are made available periodically as a result of parliamentary questions and debates. Most recently, new statistical information on the numbers of children in detention was provided during two debates in the House of Lords associated with the Asylum and Immigration (Treatment of Claimants etc) Bill.[24] The Refugee Council Children's Panel, which is funded by the Home Office to provide specialist advice to unaccompanied asylum-seeking and refugee children, collates statistical information on the cases with which it comes into contact, as do various other voluntary sector organisations and some local authorities.

There are a number of problems with the available data that make it virtually impossible to assess the extent to which children are detained in the UK or the average lengths of time spent in detention. The Government's published statistics do not include information on the total number of children detained over a period of time, the age of these children, at what stage of the family's case they were detained, nor the outcome of the detention, including whether or not these children are subsequently removed from the UK. Neither do they show the length of time for which the children are detained.

The limitations of snapshot data mean that it is not possible to identify the length of detention for either individual children or on average. For example, a child could be detained for up to 89 days and not appear in any published statistics because the detention takes place between the two snapshot dates. Since there are significant concerns about the length of time for which children are detained with no prospects of their removal, the absence of this data represents a significant gap in the evidence base. Just as significantly, there is no published Home Office data on the numbers of cases where the age of the applicant is disputed, nor the proportion or number of age-disputed individuals who are detained.

Despite these gaps in what is known about the number of children in immigration detention, Government ministers and spokespeople have repeatedly used existing snapshot statistics to argue that very few children are detained.[25] These statistics indicate that in September 2004, for example, 40 children (representing 3.6% of the total detained population) were in detention on this date.[26] Of these children, 25 had been in detention for 14 days or less, five for between 15 and 29 days, five for between one and two months, and five for between three and four months.

However, even taken on their own terms, our cumulative analysis of the available data indicates that there are significant numbers of children detained in the UK for the purpose of immigration control over time and that to suggest otherwise by reference to the snapshot data is misleading. In May 2004, Lord Bassam stated that during March and April 2004 a total of 323 children were taken into detention, half of whom were under the age of five. The average length of detention for the 323 children was four nights and 40 per cent were in detention for one night only. Of the remainder, 47 children (15 per cent) were detained for up to 14 nights, and 16 children (5 per cent) were detained for more than 14 days.[27] If the number of children detained over this two-month period were to be replicated across a 12-month period, this would mean that around 2,000 children are being detained with their families every year for the purpose of immigration control.

Quarterly snapshot statistics on the number of children in detention at any particular point in time also provide a misleading picture of the overall number of children detained in specific detention facilities. The Home Office publishes figures for the number of families detained at Oakington Reception Centre as part of NSA procedures. A composite analysis of the Home Office's published figures for Oakington over a 12-month period between September 2003 and September 2004 indicates that a total of 585 children were detained at Oakington. In addition, however, it is known that other families with children are held at Oakington as part of the Detention Overspill Facility (DOF). These families are not subject to fast track proceedings and are not included in statistics relating to Oakington. Some of these families are detained for considerable periods of time while arrangements for their removal are being made. As with the numbers of children detained across the detention estate, figures for those detained at Oakington as part of NSA procedures do not include those individuals whose age is disputed.

1.4.2 Data on age-disputed cases

The absence of any data on the number of cases in which the age of an asylum applicant is disputed is of particular concern. According to the Refugee Council, the number of cases referred to the Children's Panel that were age-disputed rose steadily between 2001 and 2003. Although annual figures have fluctuated, the actual number of referrals has not increased overall. Yet in 2001, 11 per cent of all cases referred to the Children's Panel were age-disputed; in 2002 the figure had risen to 28 per cent and in 2003, was 25 per cent.

The Children's Panel also reports an increase in the number of referrals of detained cases. Between February 2002 and January 2003, the Panel received 96 referrals of detention cases. Between February 2003 and January 2004 this number had increased to 280, of which 249 were from Oakington. This represents an increase of 292 per cent. This is of particular concern when seen in the context of evidence that a significant proportion of age-disputed individuals who are detained as adults are subsequently assessed to be children. Recent statistics collected by Cambridgeshire Social Services at Oakington Reception Centre indicate that in the 11 months between November 2003 and September 2004, 48 per cent of those age-assessed by social services were found to be under 18 years of age and released from detention. This information is supported by figures collated by the Refugee Council and Refugee Legal Centre. If this situation were to be replicated across the detention estate, it is conceivable that hundreds of separated or unaccompanied children are being detained in the UK at any one time, even though the use of detention in these circumstances contravenes existing government policy.

In addition to the problems of data specifically on the detention of children and those whose age is disputed, there are a number of other statistical issues that need to be addressed in order to establish a complete picture of the issues and the reasons why the detention of children appears to have increased:

* Removal data does not distinguish families from single adults, so that it is not possible to identify what proportion of all removals are families.
* Statistics on forced removal from the UK include dependants, whereas statistics on voluntary departure do not. Given the pressure to increase removals from the UK, this has given rise to concerns that there is less incentive to secure the return of families with children through voluntary mechanisms because these do not contribute as significantly to overall removal targets.
* As was noted earlier in this report, there is no published data on the absconding rates for asylum-seekers in general, or for families and those whose age is disputed in particular. The Home Office acknowledges that this situation is unsatisfactory.[28]

The publication of consistent and regular statistical information is essential to enable the detention of children to be properly monitored and its impacts on both children and the use of the detention estate to be accurately assessed. The availability of this information would contribute towards greater transparency in the public and political debate and enable the Home Office and HMIP to ensure that policy and practice are evidence-based.

1.5 Our evidence base

1.5.1 Research method

The research for this report began in May 2004 and was completed at the end of September 2004. The report was written between October 2004 and January 2005. We used a variety of methods to gather information, which has been triangulated to ensure consistency and robustness.

As noted above, there is limited statistical evidence relating to the detention of children on which to base an analysis of current policy and practice. Although there has been some recent research and policy analysis specifically on the detention of children,[29] this is also limited compared to the evidence base relating to UK immigration detention generally,[30] and the detention of children elsewhere.

We began our research by undertaking a comprehensive review of the existing literature. In Australia a significant amount of research and other information is now available as a result of the recent National Inquiry into Children in Immigration Detention undertaken by the Human Rights and Equal Opportunity Commission (HREOC).[31] The immigration-related detention of large numbers of children in the United States has been the focus of several reports (see, for example, Ehrenreich and Tucker 1997; Human Rights Watch 1998; Amnesty International 2003). We also examined existing research on alternatives in a number of other European countries and in the US (see, for example, ECRE 1997; Stone 2000; Justice for Asylum-seekers Alliance 2002). Most recently, UNHCR has undertaken an extensive comparative analysis on alternatives to the detention of asylum-seekers and refugees in 34 countries around the world. We understand that this study will be published in 2005. A list of the existing research and resources reviewed as part of this research and reflected in our analysis is provided at the end of this report.

Over a period of approximately three months, and using the evidence gathered through the literature review to shape our investigations, we then undertook interviews with more than 40 government officials, policy-makers, practitioners and stakeholders (Annex 1). A number of these subsequently participated in a roundtable discussion of our early findings and emerging conclusions (Annex 2). We also undertook one-day visits to Oakington Reception Centre and Dungavel House Removal Centre to observe facilities and meet with staff.

In order to gather information from children about their experiences of being detained we decided – for ethnical and practical reasons – to develop a case study approach. The case studies were produced through a variety of different methods including an analysis of information provided by Bail for Immigration Detainees (BID), pro forma questionnaires completed by Immigration Advisory Service staff at Oakington and, in a smaller number of cases, interviews with children and/or their parents who were no longer detained and had not been removed from the UK. Our research sample comprises 32 case studies. These cases consist of 25 families with children and a further seven separated children who were detained as adults because their age was disputed by the Home Office but who have subsequently been assessed to be under 18 years of age.[32] In total, 41 children are included in our case study sample, a summary of which is

provided in Annex 3. They include:

- *Children from a wide range of countries* including Togo, Jamaica (5), Belarus, South Africa (2), Cameroon (4), Brazil, Rwanda, Kosovo, Montenegro, Guinea, Nigeria (2), Albania (2), Afghanistan, Moldova, Ghana, Angola, Ukraine, Zimbabwe, Sudan, Uganda, Kyrgyzstan, and Turkey.
- *Children detained in different centres.* Although a substantial proportion of these children were detained at Oakington, some of the children in families had been detained in Dungavel and Tinsley House. A number of the children whose age was disputed had been held in Harmondsworth.
- *Children of different ages.* Just over half (51 per cent) were under five years old at the time that they were detained. Fifteen of these (36.5 per cent of the total number of children) were aged under two.[33] Included in this group were a number of very young babies, including one of 12 days and another of five weeks. Just under one-quarter of the children in our sample were aged between five and 12 years of age and the same number were aged between 13 and 17. Most of these were the children whose age was disputed. There were also two young women who were themselves unaccompanied asylum-seeking children when they arrived in the UK and subsequently had children of their own. On turning 18 they and their children were detained and removed from the UK.

We recognise that there are limitations to the case study approach. These stem both from the size of the sample involved and from the fact that it is not always possible to include 'both sides of the story'.[34] We do not claim that our case studies are representative of all detained cases not least because the characteristics of the total population of detained children are not known. Rather, the case studies are illustrative of the wide range and complexity of circumstances by which children come to be detained. We do not have enough information about each case to be able to assess the rights of and wrongs of the detention itself and that is not our objective. We are instead concerned to examine the impacts of detention on children and the alternative mechanisms that might be used to ensure compliance with immigration controls without recourse to detention. The evidence collected during the course of this research has enabled us to piece together the immigration histories of many of the children involved. This provides a useful insight into the circumstances of different cases, particularly when perceptions and experiences of detainees are triangulated against the information gathered during our interviews with stakeholders and from staff and managers at the centres. Names in the case studies have been changed to protect the identity of children and their families.

Key findings

- UK Government immigration detention policy is in breach of international legislation and guidelines. The detention of children for the purpose of immigration control runs contrary to a range of international standards relating to the treatment of children and prisoners, including the UN Convention on the Rights of the Child (UNCRC). UNHCR regards the detention of asylum-seekers as inherently undesirable and even more so in the case of vulnerable groups including children in families and unaccompanied minors.

- The UK's Reservation to the UNCRC has been widely interpreted in policy and practice to exclude asylum-seeking and other children subject to immigration control from the provisions of the UNCRC. The Reservation symbolises the relationship between law and policy in the areas of immigration and children more generally. Immigration is one of the few areas of UK law where the child's welfare is not considered to be the paramount consideration.

- The increased detention of children reflects the growing use of the detention estate to meet the objectives of UK asylum and immigration policy, including fast track processing of asylum applications and an increased emphasis on removals.

- Assessing the exact numbers of children detained in the UK and the length of time for which they are detained is impossible because of significant gaps in the evidence base. Based on existing data, we estimate that around 2,000 children are detained with their families every year for the purpose of immigration control. There is evidence that the number of age-disputed asylum-seekers has increased and that a significant proportion of those who are detained and who subsequently receive a formal age assessment are found to be children.

Recommendations

- The UK Government should review its practice in line with international standards and guidelines which state that asylum-seeking children should not be detained. The UK's Reservation to the UNCRC should be withdrawn.

- Detailed statistics on the detention of children for immigration purposes should be published on a regular basis. These statistics should include information on the overall numbers of children detained and the average length of detention. Statistics should also be published on the number of asylum applications involving age-dispute issues, including the numbers that are detained.

Notes

2 In response to an appeal from Bishop Mone on 17th July 2003 to end the detention of children seeking asylum, the Home Secretary, Rt. Hon. David Blunkett MP stated that: "detention, while regrettable, is an essential part of effective immigration control. It is in all our interests to minimise the time that children and their families remain in detention . . . I will listen to those with workable solutions to this."

3 *R (Konan) v SSHD*, CO/4926/2002 [2004] EWHC 22 Admin

4 Other relevant instruments include the UN's Standard Minimum Rules for the Treatment of Prisoners, adopted in 1955 and extended in 1977 to ensure protection for all detained persons; the 1988 Body of Principles for the Protection of All Persons under any Form of Detention or Imprisonment (BOP) and the 1990 Rules for Juveniles Deprived of their Liberty (JDL)

5 UNHCR's Guidelines on the Detention of Asylum-seekers (Revised, 26.02.99) Guideline 6

6 ibid.

7 Article 3 of the UNCRC states that "in all actions concerning children, whether undertaken by public or private social welfare institutions, courts of law, administrative authorities or legislative bodies, the best interests of the child shall be a primary consideration".

8 See Blake and Drew (2001) for further information.

9 UN Committee on the Rights of the Child, Initial Report by the UK, paras 526 et seq. Committee Report SR 204, paras 18–23

10 Article 22 of UNCRC states that 'States Parties shall take appropriate measures to ensure that a child who is seeking refugee status or who is considered a refugee in accordance with applicable international or domestic law and procedures shall, whether unaccompanied or accompanied by his or her parents or by any other person, receives appropriate protection and humanitarian assistance in the enjoyment of applicable rights set forth in the present Convention and in other international human rights or humanitarian instruments to which the said States are parties'.

11 Committee on the Rights of the Child: consideration of report submitted by the United Kingdom of Great Britain and Northern Ireland. UN Doc CRC/C/15/Add.34, Eighth Session, 1995

12 UN Committee on the Rights of the Child, Concluding Observations in the Second UK Report, para.49

13 This prioritising of immigration control over the best interests of children is a position shared by the Minister for Children, Young People and Families. See Letter and Memorandum from Margaret Hodge in response to questions raised by the Joint Committee on Human Rights in connection with the then Children Bill (June 2004), available at www.publications.parliament.uk/pa/jt200304/jtselect/jtrights/161/16109.htm

14 Available at www.official-documents.co.uk/document/cm53/5387/cm5387.pdf

15 Powers to detain asylum-seekers, including children, exist under Schedule 2 and 3 of the 1971 Immigration Act.

16 See the Ministerial Statement by Des Brown MP of 16th Sept 2004 on fast track asylum and detention policy available at www.parliament.the-stationery-office.co.uk/pa/cm200304/cmhansrd/cm040916/wmstext/40916m02.htm#40916m02.html_spmin0

17 This shift in emphasis is reflected in the re-designation of most immigration detention centres as removal centres in November 2001

18 Statement by Prime Minister Tony Blair made on 16th September 2004, available at www.ind.homeoffice.gov.uk/ind/en/home/news/press_releases/destroy_travel_documents.html

19 See Baldaccini (2004) for further information about these concerns

20 The full text of the Children Act (2004) is available online at http://www.hmso.gov.uk/acts/acts2004/20040031.htm

21 Joint Committee on Human Rights report on the Children Bill (Sept 2004), available at http://www.publications.parliament.uk/pa/jt200304/jtselect/jtrights/161/161.pdf

22 Given the location of detention facilities with family accommodation, the majority of detained children will be held in Scotland and England. A recent report by Wiesener and Corrigan (2004) indicates that some children are now being detained in some prisons in Northern Ireland.

23 Quarterly statistics are available at www.homeoffice.gov.uk/rds/immigration1.html

24 These debates took place on the 27th April 2004 www.parliament.the-stationery-

office.co.uk/pa/ld200304/ldhansrd/vo040427/text/40427-08.htm and 18th May 2004 www.parliament.the-stationery-office.co.uk/pa/ld199900/ldhansrd/pdvn/lds04/text/40518-23.htm

25 See, for example, the comments made by Lord Bassam of Brighton on 18th May 2004 in a House of Lords when he stated that: "Unfortunately, despite figures to the contrary that we have given previously, the misconception that there are large numbers of families detained for lengthy periods continues to prevail in some quarters. At any one time there are very few families in detention – something we have been saying for some time, but it is a message we must repeat." See www.parliament.the-stationery-office.co.uk/pa/ld199900/ldhansrd/pdvn/lds04/text/40518-24.htm

26 See www.homeoffice.gov.uk/rds/pdfs04/asylumq304.pdf

27 Full text available at www.parliament.the-stationery-office.co.uk/pa/ld199900/ldhansrd/pdvn/lds04/text/40518-24.htm

28 In its report on asylum removals, the Home Affairs Committee (2003, para. 65) was critical of the lack of statistical information available, including on rates of absconding, and recommended that steps be taken to remedy the situation without delay. In July 2003 the former Minister for Immigration and Citizenship, Beverley Hughes, accepted this recommendation but data on absconding rates have not yet been published.

29 See, for example, McLeish, Cutler and Stancer (2002), Cole (2003) and Refugee Council (2003)

30 See, for example, Amnesty International (1996), Pourgourides et al (1996), Weber and Gelsthorpe (2000), Barbed Wire Britain (2002), Weber and Landman (2002), and Cutler and Ceneda (2004).

31 The report of the National Inquiry into Children in Immigration Detention, along with the majority of the submissions and a number of thematic background papers can be found at www.hreoc.gov.au/human_rights/children_detention/index.html

32 Any cases that subsequently transpired to be subject to on-going disputes over age were discarded.

33 The ages of children refer to the age at which the child or children were detained rather than age at which they entered the UK or current age, unless stated otherwise.

34 For example, research by Cole (2003) has been criticised by Home Office Ministers because the number of cases exampled was small and because the report does not provide the context or the detail of the reasons why particular decisions were made in individual cases. See Hansard 8th May 2003, col. 935, available at www.parliament.the-stationery-office.co.uk/pa/cm200203/cmhansrd/vo030508/debtext/30508-32.htm#30508-32_head1

2 The impacts of detention

It is difficult to generalise about the impacts of detention because of differences between children and the circumstances under which they are detained. These differences may reflect, for example, the circumstances and experiences of children in their country of origin and in the UK and variations in the mental and physical health of children and their parents prior to detention. Pre-detention indicators are rarely available to enable the specific impacts of detention to be measured over time. While some of the impacts on children stem from detention itself, others reflect uncertainty – and possibly fear – about the immigration situation as a whole, which may be exacerbated by detention but are not wholly attributable to it.

2.1 The triple vulnerability of children

Despite these caveats, existing research and other evidence available in the UK and elsewhere suggests that while detention is an unpleasant and potentially damaging experience for anyone, the impacts on children may be particularly negative. This is because children have a triple vulnerability – as children, as detainees, and as asylum-seekers or otherwise uprooted children. Although there is some evidence from our case studies of physical consequences for children, the greatest negative impacts appear to be in terms of mental health. There is also some evidence that detention may have ongoing long-term consequences for children. The impacts on age-disputed individuals detained as adults but subsequently found to be children appear to be particularly negative.

2.2 Physical symptoms and their treatment

There is considerable research evidence that detention can have negative physical impacts on children. Physical symptoms of distress are particularly likely in young children. Australian experts have highlighted the fact that infants suffering trauma tend to present with problems of physical functioning, such as settling, feeding or sleeping difficulties, listlessness, apathy or irritability (Australian Association for Infant Mental Health 2003).

There is evidence of the physical impacts of detention on children in HMIP's most recent report on Oakington, which found that most of the 24 child protection 'cause for concern' forms opened in the previous nine months had been opened because of concerns about the child's failure to thrive, rather than suspected abuse. There was evidence in these documents of feeding and sleeping problems and depression that resulted from the trauma of removal from habitual surroundings, particularly school, or from the fact of detention itself (HMIP 2004). The evidence collected during the course of our research is consistent with that in previous research that women with young babies complained of restrictive provisions of nappies and baby milk and parents worried about their children's weight loss and conditions such as mouth infections (McLeish, Cutler and Stancer 2002; Cole 2003). The most common reported outcome is a failure to thrive, often linked to an unwillingness to eat and consequent associated weight loss. Food is one of the daily needs over which detainees do not have control – either in terms of what they eat, or when they can eat it. This factor has been reported by Cole (2003), and was reflected in the experiences of the respondents in our research, where individuals or their records reported that that their children had refused to eat properly. Shontelle, for example, commented that:

[Leah] didn't enjoy eating the food. The food was good, but she wasn't used to food like that. She would take a few chips. Sometimes she would have nothing.

Two mothers were concerned that their one-year-old babies were not eating enough. Another family expressed concern about the type of food that was available for their children Souzan (aged four) and Farouk (20 months):

The food for us and [our] kids is not good. Our kids they eat only traditional food.

Children whose age was disputed told us that one of the main problems with the food was not what was available but the fact that there were set meal times, which did not coincide with when they were hungry. For example, Bem, who was 16 when he was detained, told us:

Sometimes they would force me to eat. I was not hungry. They say it is time for food . . . [that] I have to go back to the place for eating.

The experiences of Annette and her children (see below) are illustrative of the physical impacts of detention on children, particularly where those children have been living in the UK for some time prior to their detention.

Other children in our case studies suffered from skin complaints and persistent respiratory conditions. This is most evident in those cases where children have been detained for very lengthy periods of time, particularly those in excess of 100 days.

When detainees first arrive at a removal centre, there is usually an initial assessment of physical health, which is reviewed after four weeks. The exception to this is

Annette, Lauren (aged 13) and Khamisi (aged ten)

Lauren and Khamisi came to the UK to live with their aunt in 2001 and attend school in the UK. They were ten and seven years old respectively. In 2002, their mother Annette joined them on a visa. She claimed asylum in the UK after her application for a visa extension was refused. Annette says that her legal representative failed to make a proper statement outlining the reasons for her asylum claim and when she was asked to attend an interview in June 2004 she was detained. Lauren and Khamisi were taken out of school and detained with her at Oakington. Annette's application was dealt with under NSA procedures and refused. The family remained in detention while proceedings began to obtain travel documents for the family to be returned to their country of origin.

Procedures for a bail hearing began after Annette contacted BID. As part of this process, BID arranged for an independent doctor to visit the family. The doctor found that while in detention both Annette's and her children's health had deteriorated.

Annette told BID that Lauren had been unaware of the family's immigration status and had adapted to school life in the UK. She had started secondary school and was doing well. She had been unable to say goodbye to her friends and teachers and was upset about this. She had become withdrawn and anxious, and spent her time watching television rather than attending class. Khamisi had been attending primary school prior to detention where he had settled well and had many friends. He was upset and frightened having been unable to say goodbye to his friends, and did not wish to attend the Oakington class. His mother described him as worried, and said he would go to sleep late and wake late, missing breakfast.

Annette and her children were released on Temporary Admission before the bail hearing had taken place. The family had been detained for 41 days.

for those families who are detained at Oakington as part of the Detention Overspill Facility (DOF), for whom no health assessments are carried out. Removal centre staff with whom we met during the course of this research expressed confidence in their ability to detect and act on any problems as they arise. Staff at Dungavel emphasised that the centre's surgery runs as any other surgery and we were informed that:

The medical team here work like an independent GP practice. Their allegiance is to the General Medical Council, not us.

One removal centre doctor emphasised that:

If I think when I see a child they are medically unfit to be here and I can't meet their medical needs, then I will tell the office. But it's never happened with a child.

Despite this, several of our respondents expressed a lack of confidence in the ability or willingness of medical staff to provide treatment for their complaints. Shontelle told us that there were no checks on her eight-year-old daughter Leah while they were in detention:

Those doctors in detention, they don't believe anything. They don't take your sickness seriously. My impression is they think you're lying.

Another mother reported that the migraine medicine she had been prescribed was taken away from her in detention, and that for the first month of her detention she had only been able to obtain paracetamol. In addition, an urgent operation had been planned at the time of her detention, which was consequently not carried out.

Daren was 16 years old when he was detained after travelling to the UK clandestinely on a ship. It had been a long and arduous journey taking over a month, during which time he had suffered from hunger, cold and the effects of drinking seawater. He told us that he had not received any treatment for these symptoms while in Dungavel:

I couldn't really eat, my stomach was bad, everything was blocked. After three days, I went to the doctor because I was sick, my body was not okay. He said that happens to everyone. I asked but he wouldn't give me drugs. Another day I went to the nurse but she said I should come back. But I was tired, weak.

Daren's comments reflect the findings of research in the United States, which emphasises the interdependence between physical and mental health for detainees (Physicians for Human Rights 2003). One of the difficulties in the detention context is that physical symptoms may not manifest themselves immediately on arrival or may simply be a symptom of an underlying mental anxiety which cannot be easily resolved. Problems such as pain, headaches, and gastrointestinal complaints may equally be somatic manifestations of their stressful conditions. These problems can be difficult to identify and treat because patients are effectively describing mental health problems, and the doctor is focusing on a physical health problem. This can lead to frustration on the part of both doctors and patients.

2.3 Education and learning

There is concern within the voluntary sector and among education providers that longer periods of detention can damage children's academic and social development. The educational facilities available in centres where families are detained with their children have been found to be inadequate (HMIP 2002, 2004: HMIE 2003). There are particular issues around the educational facilities available for older children aged 12 to 18 years of age, which are reflected in the concerns of parents of older children (Cole 2003). Our evidence suggests, however, that the impacts of detention on the education of children arise less from the quality of the facilities themselves and more from the disruption to existing schooling, the environment in which the education facilities are located and the impacts on future schooling when children are subsequently released. As with all other areas of our research, the fact that children whose age is disputed are treated as adults has implications for the ability to access appropriate educational services.

Jocelyn's daughter Talicia (aged ten) had been about to sit her SATS when they were detained in Dungavel. Although educational facilities in Dungavel were widely acknowledged by our research respondents to be of good quality – especially for younger children – being educated in a removal centre inevitably involves a lack of contact with peers and difficulties in tailoring provision to the different ages and needs of children. Moreover, our evidence suggests that the general and sometimes overwhelming impacts of detention on mental health undermine the ability and willingness to learn of many children.

Marcia's daughter, Sylvie (aged seven), and son, John (aged five), were also in school prior to being detained. Marcia's children were strongly affected by their time in detention. John was frustrated and teary, while Sylvie was especially anxious. She had been doing well at school and was upset at missing a planned exam and project. Both children refused to go to the classes at Oakington:

There were these classes at Oakington. The children said, 'Mummy, that's not school'. I would sometimes bring them there just so I could get some time to think. I tried really hard to look after them.

Education is sometimes regarded some as a way of 'passing time' or giving parents a break from their children rather than a learning or developmental process. Shontelle made similar comments in relation to her daughter Leah, aged eight at the time:

The only time I could have out was when she was in class. She liked it in school there. It was the only thing which got her through the day. Sometimes I needed to get away, to be alive. I thought I was going crazy.

Some stakeholders interviewed noted the particular social difficulties encountered by detained teenagers with respect to being removed from their social environment at a time when their peer group is particularly important.

It is also important to recognise that there can be long-term consequences for the education of children. Marcia told us that when she and her children were

eventually released from detention after 33 days, she informed the children's school they had been on holiday, because she did not want others to know that the family had been detained:

When we came out of detention I didn't want to tell the school why we were away. A friend of mine told them that we were on holiday. When we came back, the children's school places had gone, but that has been solved now.

This has further repercussions since teachers cannot therefore take the detention experience into account, for example if there are any learning or behavioural difficulties.

These findings suggest that, regardless of the improvements that are made to educational facilities themselves, detention has educational and learning consequences for children which cannot be controlled for and which go beyond the period of detention itself.

2.4 Impacts on mental health

Detention without time limit, no matter how reasonable the conditions, is extremely stressful. When combined with an uncertain future, language difficulties, a perceived or real lack of information and the fact that some detainees appear to be terrified at the prospect of being deported, the stress increases.

This statement by Judge Stephen Tumin, made in 1995, suggests that the impacts of being detained for the purpose of immigration control have long been recognised (Amnesty International 1996). While these impacts are by no means limited to children, there is extensive evidence of significant mental health problems in children and adolescents who are detained (see, for example, Thomas and Lau 2002; Australian Association for Infant Mental Health 2003; Australasian Society for Traumatic Stress Studies 2003; ChilOut 2002). Even without being detained, children – even more than adults – have been found to suffer prolonged psychological distress after resettlement (Thomas and Lau 2002; Silove et al 2000). Child asylum-seekers and refugees outside of detention have been found to be at greater risk of psychological problems than comparable children in the same schools (Fazel and Stein 2003). There is also evidence about the mental health impacts of detention generally, particularly where this occurs suddenly and is of an indeterminate length (Pourgourides et al 1996). Much of this evidence also suggests that mental health services are unlikely to be successful in the detention environment because detention is itself a cause of trauma and stress. In some cases we found evidence of retraumatisation where there has been previous trauma and distress in the country of origin or during transit to the UK.

Professionals to whom we spoke within removal centres recognised that the very fact of being detained can have damaging mental health implications, regardless of the quality of care that is available. As one removal centre doctor told us:

The impact of detention is based on the concept of not having freedom. [It's] control over your life, being separated from family and friends that has the greatest impact.

In this section of the report we examine the effects of a lack of information and of parent's mental health on children who are detained with their families. It also considers the mental health impacts of detention on seperated children whose age is disputed.

2.4.1 The effects of lack of information

For asylum-seekers awaiting a decision on their claim, or awaiting removal after a negative decision, the anxiety of an unknown future, including actual or perceived risk of return to the country of origin, has been linked to high levels of despair and acts of desperation (Silove et al 1993). The circumstances under which children are detained can exacerbate feelings of being out of control and may mean that the family is not mentally prepared for what is happening to them. Respondents' accounts of being taken into detention consistently referred to fear and bewilderment. Marcia's recollections of being detained with her two children aged seven and five are illustrative of this:

The lady I spoke to at Immigration set up an interview date, and said I should bring the children with me. She said one day out of school wouldn't make any difference. When we got there, the lady took us straight into a back room. She said she had learned that my case had been refused. She said we could appeal, but we could only do this [after we had left the country]. She said there was a flight booked for the next day. I was in shock. The kids were in shock too. I asked, 'How can you do this?' I was really upset and started crying and I just sat down on the floor. I asked if they would take us to the house to get some clothes, but they wouldn't.

Detention intensifies existing feelings of being out of control and is exacerbated by the lack of information associated with the asylum process in general and the decision to detain in particular. Both parents and age-disputed children in our case studies emphasised the negative impacts on their mental health of not having key information about the reasons for their detention, how long they would be detained, how to obtain release and whether their removal was imminent. The extent to which children, especially older separated children whose age is disputed, are negatively impacted by lack of information. Loss of control reflects the length of detention and is compounded by other factors, for example, the inability to access legal advice or to maintain contact with others. Several parents expressed distress at not being able to answer their children's, often-repeated, questions about why the family was being detained and when they would be released. Shontelle told us:

[Leah] was always asking me when we were leaving. I would say 'soon.' Sometimes she would look out of the window and ask over and over 'when are we leaving' and when I answered she got miserable and frowned.

Very many of our case study respondents reported that the experience of being detained had negative impacts on their children's mental health. Marcia told us that her seven-year-old daughter, Sylvie, had been particularly affected:

The children were sick in detention. My daughter

Sylvie said she was going to kill herself in there. She was crying all the time…She would be sucking her fingers and saying 'I'm going to kill myself'.

2.4.2 The effects of parents' mental health on their children

For children detained with their families, the impacts on mental health are mediated by the mental health of their parents and other adults with whom they come into contact. Children's experience of their relationship with their main carer is fundamental to their development. There is evidence that parental ill-health, overwhelming stress or social disadvantage can lead to disruption in the development of a secure attachment relationship with infants and young children. These consequences can continue on through childhood and into adult life (Australian Association for Infant Mental Health 2003). In addition, children can experience a threat to the meaning of their life if they see their parents made powerless and helpless, or made unavailable because they are depressed, irritable or otherwise disturbed themselves (Steel 2003; Zwi et al 2003). Parents' inability to protect their children from an environment of despair is damaging to both children and parents, as are parents' consequent feelings of hopelessness and guilt at their inability to provide their children with better circumstances (ChilOut 2002).

Parents with whom we spoke reported their own worsening mental health in detention and recognised the impact that this was having on their children. For example, Shontelle, who was detained with her eight-year-old daughter, Leah, said:

I thought I was going crazy. I was on anti-depressants. I am still on them. The nurse there gave me anti-depressants. I was also taking sleeping tablets because I couldn't sleep . . . In detention, I was crying. When I cried, [my daughter] cried as well. I used to feel suicidal at one point. I can see why people do it – the pressure.

The mental health of children can also be affected by the state of mind of other adults in detention. Although children in families are held in separate

---

Collette and Sandrine (aged two years)

Collette arrived in the UK in the summer of 2001, and claimed asylum on the same day. She was 16 at the time and had suffered rape, imprisonment and detention prior to leaving her country of origin. Shortly after arriving in the UK, Collette became pregnant. Sandrine was born in the spring of 2002. Until then, Collette had been cared for by social services, but after Sandrine was born she was housed in a one-bedroom flat and attended college. About one month later, Collette's asylum claim was refused, and her appeal was dismissed at the end of 2002.

In the spring of 2004, Collette and her daughter were taken to Tinsley House in order to be removed from the UK. Collette was handcuffed and extremely upset. The following morning she was woken at 3am and in spite of her resistance was taken to mainland Europe for a connecting flight to her country of origin. Collette insisted that her life would be in danger if she was returned to her country of origin, and she was brought back to the UK on the same day. A few days later another attempted removal was made, but Collette resisted and that evening she and Sandrine were taken to Oakington.

In total there were three failed removal attempts in four days, during one of which Collette reported that she was elbowed and later kicked in the stomach. BID applied for bail but bail was refused and it is thought that Collette and Sandrine were removed from the UK. They had been detained for around 60 days.

family units at both Oakington and Dungavel, the same cannot be said of those children whose age is disputed and who are detained as adults. Immigration detention, where individuals spend time in a monotonous and stressful environment, surrounded by others in the same predicament, creates the potential for a 'pressure cooker effect' of mounting despair, suspicion and frustration (Silove et al 1993). Adult detainees sometimes resort to hunger strikes in a desperate bid to have their needs addressed. Instances of self-harm and suicide attempts have increased in UK removal centres, and HMIP inspections have highlighted a lack of procedural safeguards against these risks (Baldaccini 2004). Research in Australia has found that children reported greater distress than adults in detention at witnessing acts of self-harm and suicide by other detainees (Steel 2003). Young people detained as children have reported that they viewed detention as a place where people were crazy, and that they became different people after one or two weeks (Chapman 1999).

2.4.3 Mental health of separated children

Given this context, it is perhaps not surprising that the strongest evidence of severe impacts on mental health among our case studies was on separated children whose age was disputed by the Home Office and who were treated as adults. These children find themselves in detention, separated from their parents and all other meaningful adults and completely without support. Research by Ayote and Williamson (2001) indicates that children aged 13 to 17 who have been detained in the UK are – like adult detainees – often unable to comprehend the reasons for their detention, feel criminalised and lack information about the process or its possible outcomes. One reported that his three-month detention 'was just like a year'. The children in our case studies shared these feelings.

Daren told us that after his arduous and lengthy journey to the UK, he had initially been relived to find himself in Dungavel. These feelings changed when he realised he was being detained and was given no explanation about what would happen to him. He found conditions in Harmondsworth particularly difficult:

At first I was happy but after the first or second day I saw we can't walk, just upstairs and downstairs, and I started feeling bad. Nobody explained why we were there . . . I stayed there two weeks. During that time we just feel we were not going out of the house. It was like a house, but locked . . . [Later] I was transferred to Harmondsworth . . . Harmondsworth is the worst place. All the doors are locked, that place is very tight.

Nowhere are the mental health impacts of detention on children clearer than in the case of Jacques (see page 20). The impacts of prolonged detention on Jacques' mental health are illustrative of many of the issues that emerged during the course our research. Primary among these is an overall lack of information and sense of not having any control. This is particularly evident among older children and can be exacerbated by the circumstances under which detention takes place.

In total, I spent eight months and 24 days at Harmondsworth . . . What happened at Harmondsworth – it was the hardest time of my life. It's hell. Prison is better than detention . . . In prison, you have rights, not veiled rights. In detention, you have no rights . . . The emergency numbers are barred on the phone there. I know because once somebody committed suicide – a Turkish man – and we tried to dial the emergency number and we couldn't. Everywhere there are keys, you have to be collected and taken for everything. It was very, very hard. I was hearing noises in my head . . .
(Jacques, 17)

In addition, it is clear that some children who are detained have previous experiences which make them vulnerable to re-traumatisation. Several children had experienced arduous journeys and fear. Some of these children are known to have been subject to, or to have witnessed, violence. The failure to take these issues into account when deciding to detain children and in reviews of that decision are discussed in detail in Section Four of this report.

Jacques (aged 17 years)

Jacques is from an African country. Before coming to the UK, he had been detained after the authorities came looking for his mother, whose religious activities they disapproved of. As a result of what happened to him during this time in prison and subsequently, Jacques had mental health problems before arriving in the UK, for which he took prescribed medication.

He arrived in the UK when he was 16 years old and, after sleeping rough in Croydon over the weekend, he claimed asylum on the first working day after his arrival. His age was disputed from the time of his screening interview and he was referred to the Refugee Council's Children's Panel. Although he was supported by social services, the Home Office did not accept that he was a child.

When his application for asylum was refused, Jacques attended an appeal hearing at the IAA . Despite the fact that Jacques was being supported by social services, the adjudicator came to the conclusion that Jacques was over 18 because of his physical appearance, and his appeal was dismissed. The negative outcome of his asylum application had a detrimental impact on Jacques' mental health, which deteriorated rapidly and was exacerbated by the fact that his medication had run out. On one occasion, he was unable to report as he was too ill. Despite providing evidence of his illness, Jacques was detained about one month later and after two nights in a police cell, then two at Tinsley House, he was transferred to Harmondsworth where he remained for nearly nine months.

During his time in Harmondsworth, Jacques' mental health deteriorated further still, but rather than being released or hospitalised he was segregated for his own safety and that of other inmates. After around six months in detention, Jacques was revisited by an advisor from the Refugee Council Children's Panel. As a result of this visit, he was moved to the hospital section within Harmondsworth where he remained for a further two and a half months. Eventually his solicitor made an application for bail and Jacques was released and taken back into the care of social services. He is receiving medication for his mental health problems but remains very vulnerable.

2.5 Transfers between centres

There are a number of different reasons why children may be transferred between reception and removal centres, including in order to facilitate their removal from the UK. Although transfers are in principle kept to a minimum, our research raises concerns about movements around the detention estate and the lengths of time spent in transit. These concerns are shared in HMIP's (2002) inspection of Dungavel, which concluded that transfers around the detention estate increase detainees' vulnerability.[35]

More than one-third of our case studies had been transferred between different centres. In seven cases, at least two transfers were made, meaning that these children were held in three different locations during the course of their detention. One child, Daren, was transferred five times (see box opposite).

Unexpected, unexplained, and sometimes frequent transfers between centres can also cause distress, disorientation and loss of contact between detainees and their families, friends and legal representatives (Baldaccini 2004). Bem was 16 when he arrived in the UK. He was told to lie about his age and to say that he was over 18. He was initially detained at Dungavel but subsequently transferred to Oakington and then

Harmondsworth. He described feeling disorientated by the repeated transfers:

They said they would take me to hospital. The day they said they would take me to hospital is the day they came to wake me to go to England [from Dungavel]. It was after five days. I was very weak, I was just sleeping when they came to get me. I said why am I going to England? I didn't want to go to England. But they said the authorities said we should. I said I was weak and wanted treatment. It was night when we drove to England. There were others with me. When we got there they said it was Oakington. First they said we were going to Harmondsworth but when we got there it was locked and we went to Oakington. When we got there it was two in the morning. They came around three in the morning and said we were going to Harmondsworth. They took me there in the morning. We arrived at about 11 am, or noon. I said 'why?' They said, another place. I felt sad, I didn't know what to do.

In addition, the journey between Dungavel and other detention or removal centres (including Harmondsworth, Tinsley House and Oakington) was described as being very distressing and uncomfortable by a number of children, particularly those who were being treated as adults. Daren, for example, described one of his five transfers:

I stayed in Dungavel about two weeks. One early morning they woke me up. They said I was going. They put us in a van. They told me the name of the place where we were going but I didn't know the name. The van went from early morning to 11 at night. I needed to pee but they said no, can't stop. They stopped the van to change drivers, but not to let us pee. We had a bottle of water – we threw out the water and peed in the bottle. We were six in the van. We arrived at night. They took us to one place, but they couldn't open the gate, so we went off again . . . to Oakington.

HMIP have expressed particular concerns about the length and the stress of the journeys to and from Dungavel noting that, "particularly for families, a 400-mile trip in an escort van, with escort staff reluctant to stop for comfort breaks, meant that they arrived at the centre distressed and disoriented" (HMIP 2002: 5). The evidence collected during the course of our research leads us to conclude that further action needs be taken to monitor and significantly reduce transfers generally, and in particular those involving children.

Daren (aged16 years)

Daren had just turned 16 when he arrived in Glasgow early in 2004 after a long and arduous journey to the UK. Daren was told to give immigration officers who interviewed him a date of birth which would make him over 18 years old. Although he subsequently informed removal centre staff that he was a child, no independent age assessment was undertaken and he was treated as an adult. Daren was taken to Dungavel but after two weeks was transferred to Oakington, where he stayed for one week before being transferred again, this time to Tinsley House, and then shortly afterwards, to Harmondsworth.

After his asylum application was refused, an attempt was made to remove Daren from the UK but he insisted he was a child and was taken off the plane and returned to Tinsley House after the captain of the aircraft intervened. At Tinsley House, Daren made contact with the visitor's group who put him in contact with the Refugee Council's Children's Panel. Daren was age-assessed and found to be under 18. After 55 days in detention, Daren was released into the care of social services. He now shares a flat with other teenagers and attends a local college.

2.6 Long-term consequences

The mental health impacts discussed in this section can have long-term consequences for the future of children in terms of whether they are able to pursue their applications to remain in the UK and what happens to them when they are eventually released or removed.

Among the mental health impacts of detention are concentration impairment as well as impairment of the abilities to solve problems and evaluate options, impacts of trauma such as anxious thoughts, low self-esteem and fragmented memories. In addition, the detention environment can intensify asylum-seekers' fear and mistrust of authorities.

This combination of impacts can result in difficulties in presenting clear accounts, affecting both the ability of both families and age-disputed children to pursue their applications and, in some cases, undermining the credibility of asylum-seekers' accounts of their experiences. The experience of being detained can also lead asylum-seekers to abandon their claims, even if it may not be safe for them to return to their country of origin (Pistone 1999). For children who are in families, this impact will be mediated through the effect of detention on their parents and the ability of the family as a whole to pursue legal options and access legal safeguards.

There is also research evidence – mainly from Australia – that detention can have long-term consequences for children who are eventually released and return to the community (Silove et al 2000). It should not be assumed that following release the impacts of detention will simply fall away. These experiences become part of a general pool of experience and disorders can 'erupt' after release, when immediate survival issues have receded. Anxieties, depressions, stress disorders, abuse, violence, suicidal tendencies and other phenomena may be acute, delayed or chronic.

Parents detained with their children in the UK have expressed serious concern about the immediate and long-term effects of detention on their children, with

some worrying that the fear and mistrust they saw in their children would be permanent (Cole 2003). Previous research by Save the Children has found that young people who had previously been detained felt their whole experience of the UK had been marked by their detention experience (Ayote and Williamson 2001). The length of time spent in detention, the circumstances and conditions of detention and the prior mental and physical health of both parents and children are factors influencing the long-term impacts of detention itself.

Although the long-term consequences of detention are not a focus of our research, a number of our case studies suggest that detention has ongoing negative impacts, particularly for the mental health of children. The experiences of Sofia, Visar and their son, Michael, (see page 23) are illustrative of these consequences.

Although the family have since been granted leave to remain in the UK, the experience of being taken in detention has clearly had long-term consequences for Michael, which were described to us by his mother Sofia:

> *After the detention Michael was in a bad way. The bedwetting was a problem again and he had nightmares. He wouldn't go upstairs without me. At 9pm when I took him to bed, I had to go to bed as well because he wouldn't let me leave . . . Michael was afraid of the police coming again. He was always afraid. He kept asking questions like 'what if they come and you are not in . . . will they come and get me at school?' . . . Now he is better. It took a long time for him to get better, about a year and a half. It was one year ago we had the good news. We won our appeal on human rights. [Michael] was so happy when we got the good news about the appeal, but his problems continued for some time afterwards. He continued going to the hospital for counselling for a while.*

Marcia reported similar difficulties in her daughter, Sylvie's, ability to return to normal life after being released from detention. As was described earlier in this section, Sylvie had become very depressed while in detention. Her mother told us:

Sofia, Visar and Michael (aged seven years)

Sofia and Visar travelled by lorry from an Eastern European country with their son Michael, who was five years old at that time. They arrived in the UK early in March 2000, after a long and difficult journey. Before they left their country, the family had suffered direct threats to their safety, and Michael had heard his parents being threatened. The couple claimed asylum a few days after they arrived. They were required to report and missed only one reporting date over a period of 18 months, due to Visar's ill-health.

The family was refused asylum and lodged an appeal but shortly afterwards eight or nine officers came to the family's home early in the morning to detain the family prior to their removal from the UK. Visar explained that they were waiting for an appeal date, and showed the officers a letter from their solicitor confirming this. Although able to persuade the officers not to detain his wife and child, Visar was taken into detention but released three days later.

After his father had been detained, Michael became very anxious. He was scared of coming downstairs and developed a problem with bedwetting for which he was referred to a local hospital. Michael began attending fortnightly counselling sessions and was beginning to feel less anxious when, early in 2002, while still waiting for an appeal date, the family was again woken early in the morning by a number of officers, who detained the entire family in order that they could be removed.

The family was taken to Harmondsworth and were subsequently transferred to Tinsley House where they were told they were to be removed the following morning. They were unable to contact their solicitor. At 3am the next morning the family were woken but were taken back to Harmondsworth, where they remained for several days. The family were then released. Sofia and Visar were given no explanation for the detention and attempted removal other than that there had been a mistake.

Until now [Sylvie] is still not really back to normal. I have problems with her. She's more demanding, shouting. Sometimes she's even screaming in her sleep. She wasn't like that before. Sometimes when I talk to her she doesn't listen to me, and she wasn't like that before.

We also found evidence that the impacts of detention on the mental health of parents can combine with ongoing uncertainty about their immigration status and therefore have negative effects on the quality of family life over the longer term. As Shontelle told us:

Every day is so long for me now. My children don't like it. Sometimes I can't even eat, sometimes for a week. I'm not even spending much time with the

children now, I'm finding it hard to do these things. I'm not myself right now.

For some of the separated children we spoke to, the long-term consequences of detention have been exacerbated by the loss of previous support networks. These children have already become separated from their parents and other family members. Jacques told us that he had found it very difficult to rebuild his life after being detained for nearly nine months, not least because was now living in a different area:

Since my release I've been taken into the care of social services again, but now I'm living in [a different place] and I am finding it very hard. I feel very alone and have no one to talk to . . . I am taking medicines now, four different kinds throughout the day and they help. I sleep better. It's confusing since I came out of detention though. I had to change everything . . . where I live, my doctor. I am too far to see the people I met before detention. I really need to talk to people. I find it very hard to have everything inside me and not talk.

It is clear from the evidence presented in this section that the impacts of detention, while varied, complex and difficult to measure, are often negative and never positive. For children detained with their families, the ability of parents and other carers to deal with the circumstances in which they find themselves will often determine whether or not children are able to cope with the experience. For separated children whose age is disputed and who find themselves in detention, there is no protection from a whole range of negative impacts, particularly in relation to mental health. For both groups of children these impacts will be exacerbated by a number of factors, most notably the circumstances in which the detention takes places and the length of time that it lasts.

Given the strength of this evidence about the negative impacts of detention on children, it is vital that alternatives to detention are developed which enable contact to be maintained without jeopardising the welfare of children. It is to this issue that our report now turns.

Key findings

- Children detained under immigration powers are triply at risk of negative impacts due to their vulnerabilities as children, as detainees, and as asylum-seekers or otherwise uprooted children. The greatest negative impacts appear to be in terms of mental health and these impacts may be long term. The impacts on age-disputed individuals detained as adults but subsequently found to be children are particularly negative.

- Physical symptoms include refusal to eat properly, or eating an unbalanced diet, persistent coughs and other sickness. There is a lack of confidence among detainees in the ability and willingness of detention centre medical staff to treat their symptoms or those of their children.

- The very fact of being detained can have damaging mental health implications, regardless of the quality of care that is available. Impacts on children include depression, changes in behaviour and confusion. Detention intensifies existing feelings of being out of control and is exacerbated by the lack of information associated with the asylum process in general and the decision to detain in particular. Some children have experiences which make them vulnerable to re-traumatisation. The mental health of children can also be affected by other adults' state of mind in detention, including that of parents and carers.

- Detention has educational and learning consequences for children that cannot be controlled for and which go beyond the period of detention itself. As these impacts are related to the overall detention environment, they will occur regardless of any improvements that are made to educational facilities themselves.

- Although transfers are in principle kept to a minimum, more than one-third of our case studies had been transferred between different centres. Unexpected, unexplained, and sometimes frequent transfers between centres can exacerbate mental health impacts and can cause distress, disorientation and loss of contact between detainees and their families, friends and legal representatives. Movements around the detention estate and the lengths of time spent in transit exacerbate the negative impacts of detention on children and increase their vulnerability.

Recommendations

- Because of the negative physical, mental and educational consequences of detention, children should not be detained for the purpose of immigration control. Alternatives should be developed for ensuring compliance where this is considered necessary.

- Further action needs be taken to monitor and significantly reduce transfers between different detention centres, particularly where these involve children.

Notes

35 See also HMIP's report on Campsfield House Immigration Removal Centre (September 2004), available at www.homeoffice.gov.uk/docs4/irccampsfieldhouse04.pdf

3 A measure of last resort?

Given the evidence about the negative impacts of detention presented in the previous section, the use of immigration detention should be avoided, particularly in cases involving children. Although this is accepted in principle by the Home Office, there is evidence that in practice the detention of children is not being used as a measure of last resort.

Children in families, for example, may be detained as part of fast track or accelerated procedures for asylum determination. There is also some concern among stakeholders that the Government's overall objective of increasing removal numbers and the fact that dependents are included in the removal statistics mean that families may be more rather than less likely to be detained than those without children. These stakeholders also pointed to the fact that there is particular pressure to remove families for whom the associated support costs are higher. Moreover, they suggested to us that it is often easier to locate families because they are more likely to access services for their children, particularly educational and health services. Although the suggestion that families are 'targeted' has been strongly refuted by the Home Office, this last point is of particular concern because it implies that the rationale for detaining families may sometimes be that they are less rather than *more* likely to abscond.

This section examines the factors that influence a decision to detain in particular cases and the mechanisms in place for ensuring that this decision is only taken when all other alternatives have been exhausted. Given the particularly negative impacts associated with the detention of separated children whose age is disputed, we also examine the mechanisms for ensuring that these children are not detained.

3.1 The decision to detain

IND's Operational Enforcement Manual (OEM) sets out the criteria that should be considered when making a decision about whether or not to detain. According to Chapter 38 of the OEM, there is a presumption in favour of temporary admission or temporary release.[36] Detention should only be used as a matter of last resort where there are no alternatives for ensuring compliance with immigration proceedings, including removal directions, and where there are strong grounds for believing that a person will not comply with conditions of temporary admission or release. Once detention has been authorised, it must be kept under close review to ensure that it continues to be justified.

3.1.1 Fast track procedures

Although there is a policy emphasis on using the detention estate primarily for those individuals who are at the end of the decision-making process and can be removed, many of the children in our case studies had been detained as part of fast track or accelerated procedures for asylum determination. The use of detention in order to facilitate speedier processing of asylum applications has been the subject of considerable debate, particularly in NSA cases where an appeal from within the UK is not possible. The justification for this use of detention at the beginning of the process has always been that it is usually for a short period of time.

Of the ten cases within our case study sample who were detained as part of fast track procedures, three were detained for seven days. Of the remaining seven cases, however, the detention of children for the purpose of fast track processing lasted considerably longer. One family was detained for 13 days, there were three cases where detention lasted for upwards of 40 days and three cases where detention lasted for more than 100 days. Two of the families were removed from the UK after they had been detained for 42 days and 162 days respectively. The remainder were released on Temporary Admission after extensive periods of time in detention.

These cases raise significant concerns about the possibility that children who are detained for what is intended to be a short period while the family's application for asylum is assessed can actually remain in detention for much longer periods of time.

The purpose of the fast track procedures is primarily administrative convenience. The children involved are not subject to Removal Directions at the time that the that the decision to detain is made and there is rarely any evidence to suggest that they would not comply with the conditions of Temporary Admission if they were not detained. On this basis, we conclude that there is no justification for the use of fast track procedures for cases involving children, regardless of whether these are children in families or separated children whose age is disputed. For children in families, detention is simply not a measure of last resort. And the risks of detaining age-disputed asylum-seekers who are potentially children with adults in a secure environment are too high to be justified by administrative expediency.

3.1.2 Detention prior to removal

Different issues arise where IND needs to make a decision about whether to detain a child later in the asylum process. Although additional criteria for detaining families have not been published, IND maintains that it has improved its procedures to ensure that those children who are detained with their families are detained for the shortest possible time prior to removal, for example, by ensuring that Removal Directions are in place and there are no known barriers to removal. Responsibility for ensuring that this process is effective lies with the Management of Detained Cases Unit (MODCU).

Yaryna and Vanko (aged 12 days)

Yaryna came to the UK from an Eastern European country at the end of 2003. She arrived on a visitor's visa which was valid for three months, although she intended to claim asylum. Yaryna became pregnant about a month after her arrival, before the visa expired. She had a difficult pregnancy. She went to the Home Office several times while she was pregnant, but was told to wait or come back at a different time, which she was unable to do because she was ill.

Vanko was born in July 2004. Eleven days later, Yaryna went to the Home Office and claimed asylum. She was detained with her son the following day and taken to Oakington. Yaryna obtained her first legal advice at this time but her asylum claim was refused just over a fortnight after she was first detained with her baby. Yaryna contacted BID who applied for bail. She had sureties and an address to be released to.

The hearing was listed for a date 47 days after the family were detained. BID faxed representations to MODCU and was told that this information had been forwarded to Oakington where it would be dealt with accordingly. BID requested details of MODCU's review file on the case but was told to contact Oakington about the case. Eventually BID was able to speak to MODCU's family team and was told that the family's detention had been reviewed after ten days, then again after 28 days, and every seven days since that time. The most recent review had taken place the previous day, and MODCU was satisfied that despite the delay in obtaining emergency travel documents for Vanko, the continued detention of mother and child was appropriate The following day, Yaryna and Vanko were released from detention. They had been at Oakington for 43 days.

Among our case studies there was evidence of some families being detained despite there being outstanding aspects of the asylum application. In one case, a family had an unheard appeal when they were detained on two separate occasions. The family were subsequently granted leave to remain in the UK.

The experiences of Yaryna and Vanko, detailed on page 27, also raise issues about the process of reviewing the decision to detain, which are discussed in detail later in this report.

3.1.3 Detention without full information

In other cases, a lack of information about the asylum process itself, combined with inadequate or non-existent legal advice and representation, meant that issues that were relevant to the asylum decision had not come to light or been fully considered when the decision was made to detain the family. In these cases, the need to reconsider aspects of the application while the family is in detention can mean that children are detained unnecessarily.

In one case a family was detained before any investigations had been made about whether or not

they could be removed, despite evidence that they would comply with immigration controls:

These cases raise important questions about the extent to which the Home Office is following its own procedures for making decisions about whether or not a family should be detained. There appears to be a disjuncture between the policy rationale for detaining children and operational criteria that enable it to happen in practice. These concerns are shared by HMIP, which recently concluded that decisions to detain children at Oakington did not appear to have followed even the provisions set out by the IND Operational Enforcement Manual (HMIP 2004: paragraph 9.4):

The guidance also makes clear that decisions to detain families with children should take into account Article 8 of the European Convention on Human Rights (the right to family and private life). This should therefore involve consideration of the child's interests and welfare, balanced against the necessity and length of detention. We were concerned to see no evidence of such policies and procedures in relation to children detained at Oakington. There was no evidence of external authorisation of their detention; indeed on-site immigration staff, to whom we spoke, appeared

Evelyn, Charles and their son Gerald (aged two years)

Evelyn and Charles came to the UK as students from an African country in 2000. They each had student visas that have been renewed several times. Evelyn is studying nursing and Charles is training to be an accountant. Their son Gerald was born in 2002.

In 2004, the couple went with Gerald to the French Embassy in London. They wanted to go to Paris to celebrate Gerald's second birthday. They took their passports, student visas and other documentation with them. When they arrived they were asked by staff to wait and, at the end of the day, UK Immigration Officers arrived to interview them. The family was told that the stamps on their student visas were false, and taken to Oakington.

Removal Directions were set for eight days after they were detained. The couple contacted BID. They emphasised that they had been living in the UK for nearly five years and did not understand why they were being removed when they were in the middle of their studies, and whilst they had 'contracts, loans, credit card bills to pay', as well as furniture and all their belongings in the UK. The family requested a copy of the BID Bail Notebook to apply for bail themselves but were released after ten days. They have received no further information about why they were detained.

unaware of IND's guidance on the subject, or of any specific criteria in relation to the detention of children. Nor was there any space on the proforma screening form for any assessment of risk in relation to children.

Her Majesty's Chief Inspector of Prisons, Ann Owers, concluded that instructions about the detention of children did not appear to be followed, nor to be understood, and recommended that the existing procedures and criteria for the detention of children should be rigorously implemented and monitored.

3.2 Pastoral visits and case reviews

One example of this gap between policy and practice in the process through which a decision to detain is made is the so-called 'pastoral visit', which is intended to ensure that all factors are taken into account in detaining children and that there are no unanticipated barriers to removal. In July 2001 a best practice document on how to conduct family removals was published by IND. According to IND's published instructions:

[I]t can be very helpful to visit the family to establish their current circumstances, and to assess the possibility of compliance with self-check-in removal directions. It is also possible to do this by inviting them for interview . . . During either a pastoral visit or an interview you should discuss their situation, identify any factors that might prevent or delay removal – hospital appointments, pregnancy, exceptional educational needs, and other things of this sort. This will allow you to enquire about the facilities to meet these needs in the country to which it is planned to remove the family, and to refer for further consideration cases where removal may cause serious hardship.

3.2.1 Changes in pastoral visits

According to recent correspondence between the IS Enforcement Policy Unit and Asylum Policy Stakeholders Group, this best practice document has

been considerably revised and updated over the past year. The revised guidance – which will be included as a specific chapter of the OEM which is currently being updated – appears to shift the emphasis of the pastoral visit away from ensuring that the family is aware of what will happen to them and that there are no obstacles to removal, towards ensuring that there are no obstacles to detention taking place:

There has been a Ministerial undertaking that pastoral visits should be undertaken prior to all family detention visits. Pastoral visits allow for the gathering of information regarding the circumstances of the family concerned and ensure that important issues such as medical or special needs are taken into account when deciding on arrest, detention, transportation and/or removal. Where there is good reason to suggest that a pastoral visit would adversely affect our attempts at removal (e.g. if there is evidence to suspect that the family may abscond following a pastoral visit), a written report or file minute detailing the reasons for the suspicion, must be submitted to an Immigration Inspector (HMI). The HMI will then decide whether or not the pastoral visit should be undertaken.[37]

As a result of this shift in emphasis, pastoral visits often do not take place, as it is assumed that a family will abscond if they know that removal is imminent. This means that any change in circumstances will not then be known about and the family concerned will be unaware of what is going to happen to them and unable to prepare themselves and their children accordingly.

There is no published data available about how often the decision to detain is informed by a pastoral visit. Neither is there any information available about the frequency with which it is decided that detention is either unnecessary or inappropriate as a result of a pastoral visit. The evidence collected through our case studies suggests that pastoral visits are often not carried out, and that when they are, their pastoral nature is outweighed by their use as a means of acquiring intelligence to effect detention.

Only two of the families in our case studies are known

to have received pastoral visits. In one case, comments made by the family at the time of the pastoral visit that they did not want to return to their country of origin was referred to by the Home Office in opposing bail. This was in spite of the fact that the bail summaries acknowledged that the family had previously complied. In another case, the family received a pastoral visit during the course of which it was established that the mother was pregnant with her second child. Detention for the purposes of removal was effected without a further pastoral visit seven months later, when the family's youngest baby was six weeks old. The mother was suffering serious postpartum problems for which she had an operation scheduled. The family was detained for 26 days before being removed from the UK.

HMIP (2002, 2004) is critical of the fact that IND provides families with little or no notice of removal plans on the assumption that they will abscond if they are provided with any explanation of what is about to happen to them and their children. Our case studies indicate that such an approach causes both practical and emotional problems, especially if families have lived in the UK for a number of years and are vulnerable. The experiences of Marcia and her children are illustrative of these problems (see below).

3.3 Circumstances of detention

A note of March 2004 produced by the Home Office on the collection of children from schools by immigration officers involved in family removal work

Marcia, Sylvie (aged seven years) and John (aged five years)

Marcia came to the UK at the end of 2000 and her daughter, Sylvie, and son, John, joined her after about one year. It was only when her children arrived and were given Temporary Admission that Marcia sought legal advice about her immigration status, after which she claimed asylum. She was required to report until her case was decided and she did so once a month.

Marcia's asylum claim was refused, as was her appeal. Assuming her case had been decided, she stopped reporting. Marcia was supported by family and friends and was not receiving any accommodation or subsistence from the National Asylum Support Service (NASS). Her children attended primary school, and were registered with a GP. Marcia no longer had a legal representative.

Marcia moved house because the friends with whom she was staying could no longer afford their rent. The Home Office tried to visit her at her old address and left a message asking her to contact them. When she did, she was asked to an interview with her children where she was told that her claim had been refused and that they were to be returned to their country of origin the next day. Marcia's request that they be able to collect some clothes from their home was refused and the family remained in the same clothes for three days.

Two days after their detention, the family was taken to the airport. Marcia resisted removal and the family were brought back to Oakington. Marcia instructed a new solicitor who applied for judicial review (JR). A further removal attempt was aborted as a result of the JR. After contacting BID, a bail hearing was listed but Marcia was not brought to the hearing as detention staff told her that they had no record of it. In her absence Marcia was granted bail pending additional information from her surety but was subsequently released on Temporary Admission before this information was provided. The family had been detained for 33 days.

recognises the difficulties and upset caused to staff and pupils in schools. There is no acknowledgement, however, of the impacts on the children who are being taken into detention. Once in detention, families with children may be taken from their rooms in the early hours of the morning to be removed from the UK. As a result they have no opportunity to contact other family members or their legal representatives (Cole 2003; Baldaccini 2004).

This evidence leads us to conclude that the processes for ensuring that all possible obstacles to removal are identified by MODCU prior to the decision being taken to detain a family are not always effective. This increases the risk that children will be detained unnecessarily or without any imminent prospect of their removal. There is a danger that where a review of the family's case file is undertaken by IND staff in MODCU – who are detached from the circumstances of the particular case – possible obstacles to removal or factors which make detention unnecessary or inappropriate may not be taken into account.

It is therefore our conclusion that case reviews are a key mechanism for safeguarding against the inappropriate or unlawful detention of children. The most effective way of ensuring that the decision to detain children is a fully informed one is to ensure that those with ultimate responsibility for the decision to detain – namely enforcement officers working on the ground – are able to access the family's case file at first hand and undertake a pastoral visit that is genuinely aimed at ensuring all the relevant factors are taken into account. This would reduce the possibility of the decision to detain becoming detached from the reality of the family's circumstances.

Any decision to detain must further consider how to avoid detention of children taking place from school, or early morning detentions where families wake to enforcement officers at the door and are given little time to collect their belongings. These measures can most effectively be implemented in a context of the alternatives to detention that are discussed in Section Four.

3.4 Ensuring that separated children are not detained

The evidence presented in Section Two of this report raises very significant concerns about the detention of separated children whose age is disputed by the Home Office. Although Home Office policy is to give age-disputed cases the benefit of the doubt and to treat them as children unless there is evidence that *strongly* suggests that they are over 18, the evidence collected during the course of our research indicates that this is not necessarily the case in practice and that there is a notable absence of mechanisms for ensuring that children whose age is disputed are not detained.[38]

None of the limited mechanisms that have been put in place for ensuring that the decision to detain children in families is a measure of last resort apply in cases involved age-disputed individuals. Neither do these children benefit from any of the safeguards for preventing the prolonged detention of such children that are discussed in Section Five. They are detained as adults and therefore share communal sleeping arrangements with other adults and receive no educational or other support. These individuals, a significant proportion of whom are subsequently found to be children, are therefore exceptionally vulnerable. Some of them will never get a proper assessment of their age and therefore will be at risk of being removed from the UK as separated children through fast track procedures.

3.4.1 Age assessments

The age of an individual asylum-seeker is often disputed when they first come into contact with the immigration authorities. It is currently sufficient for an immigration officer or IND caseworker to dispute a child's age based on their impression of physical appearance.[39] In some cases children may say that they are older than they are. This was the case for two of the children in our sample. From the point at which an individual's age is judged to be over 18, the onus is on that individual and his or her representative, if they have one, to seek an age assessment.

Individuals whose age is disputed are liable to be detained at Oakington (if it is a fast track case) or elsewhere if there are more general concerns about the individual's identity or compliance with the terms of Temporary Admission. Although the OEM places an obligation on the Immigration Service to refer disputed minors to the Refugee Council Children's Panel, in practice this does not always happen (Stanley 2001; ILPA and BID 2003). Even where referrals do take place, the Children's Panel does not have the resources to ensure swiftly that all, or even most, age-disputed asylum applicants are professionally age-assessed.

Instead, the Panel prioritises detained cases where contact has been made by a visitor's group, or by the Refugee Council office in Oakington, or if the claimant makes contact himself or herself. Separated children who find themselves in detention are unlikely to be able to make this contact. Our evidence indicates that this is particularly the case if they are detained in centres other than Oakington where there is an awareness of this problem and where all applicants have on-site legal advice and representation.

Although it is beyond the scope of our research to examine the complex issue of age assessment in detail, nonetheless it is important to note that this issue has become a very significant one in the immigration context over recent months. There is evidence from Oakington, referred to in Section One of this report, that a significant proportion of those who are independently assessed by social services are found to be under 18 years of age.

Among our case studies are five children whose age was disputed but who were assessed by Cambridgeshire Social Services to be under the age of 18. One of these, Farzin, arrived in the UK in July 2004 and claimed asylum on the day he arrived. He was 17. His age was disputed by an IND caseworker on the basis of his physical appearance and four days later he was sent to Oakington. Here, Farzin's legal representatives asked both Cambridgeshire Social Services and an experienced paediatrician to carry out age assessments and both concluded that he was the age that he stated. Farzin was referred to the Refugee

Council Children's Panel and released into the care of social services.

There is also evidence that even when social service assessments are undertaken, these are not always of a satisfactory standard. Concerns about the quality of age assessments undertaken by social services and the willingness or otherwise of IND to accept these where it is concluded that an age-disputed individual is a child, are reflected in several important recent legal rulings in the courts. These include age assessments carried out by Merton Social Services[40] and Enfield Social Services.[41] The evidence emerging from cases such as these has led some of those working with children to raise concerns about social services carrying out age assessments because they also have a responsibility to look after those individuals who they assess to be children. Some stakeholders whom we interviewed suggested this potential conflict of interests has been further exacerbated by the Hillingdon judgment, which established that asylum-seeking children who have formerly been looked after by a local authority are entitled to a continuing duty of care under the Children (Leaving Care) Act 2000 and should be provided with a number of services.[42] As a result, the costs associated with assessing an individual as being under 18 years of age now extend beyond his or her 18th birthday.

These concerns were reflected in the comments made during our interviews by social service practitioners, who told us that the time and effort associated with undertaking the age assessment itself are significant. There is evidently a view within the social service profession that social services are being expected to undertake age assessments of asylum-seekers for which they are neither adequately trained nor financially reimbursed by the Home Office.

Of equal concern, given our focus on ensuring that separated children are not detained, is the evidence from our research that despite an explicit and stated Home Office policy to take social service assessments into account where these consider an individual to be under 18 years of age, this is not always the case in practice. The example of Flamur illustrates this (see page 33).

Flamur (16 years old when initially detained, then re-detained aged 17 years)

Flamur arrived in the UK in 2002. He went to social services the day after he arrived in the country, and claimed asylum less than a fortnight later. He had no passport, but did have his birth certificate with him, which showed that he was 16 years old when he arrived. Flamur's age was disputed after a screening interview and he was taken to Oakington, where he was detained for six days. During this time he was interviewed, in the presence of his representative and a member of the Refugee Council's Children's Panel. His asylum claim was refused and his age continued to be disputed. When he was released, however, he was accepted by social services as being the age he said he was and supported by the local authority.

Flamur was enrolled on an ESOL course and mixed well with other students. His ESOL teacher confirmed to social services that there was no reason to doubt his stated age. He was subsequently accepted as being under 18 years of age by both an adjudicator and the Immigration Appeal Tribunal (IAT) and it was agreed that he would not be returned until he was 18. The Home Office then detained Flamur in order to remove him while he was still 17 and disputed the age assessments, stating that it was not bound by rulings by the IAA or social services. Flamur was detained for ten days before being released on Temporary Admission, following an application for bail made by BID.

3.4.2 The need for clearer procedures for age assessments

Given this evidence about the problems associated with current safeguards for ensuring that separated children are not detained, our analysis of alternatives in this area focuses on ensuring that age assessments are carried out in a timely and appropriate manner. Separated children must also be provided with care and protection while the age assessment is undertaken, and beyond. Without this, children subject to immigration control will remain vulnerable and will fall through the gaps in current provision in exactly the ways that were identified in *Every Child Matters* (DfES 2003).

There is an urgent need for clearer procedures for assessing the age of those who say that they are children but whose age is disputed by the Home Office. The momentum towards establishing such procedures has been reinforced by the case of a separated child (A) who was detained unlawfully after his age was disputed by an IND caseworker and no formal age assessment was undertaken.[43] One of the important features of the case was that the assessment of A's age as 16, plus or minus two years, made it *more*

likely that he was a minor than he was an adult by a ratio of 4:1 (Blake and Kilroy 2004).

This case and the other evidence we have considered suggests that *at a very minimum* a mechanism needs to be established to ensure that all social service departments use the same framework for age assessment. This mechanism should not be reliant upon individual cases being brought before the courts. No decision to detain should be made unless and until an age assessment has been undertaken by social services which finds an individual to be over 18 years of age.

Better still, in order to ensure that age assessments are initiated as quickly as possible and are truly independent from the consequences of the decision that is taken, an independent panel should be established which is tasked with the role of undertaking assessments of age quickly and consistently. This body should have representation from independent social workers, experienced paediatricians and multi-sector agencies. The establishment of the panel should be undertaken with the consensus and support of statutory and voluntary organisations in order to ensure that only one set of criteria is used for the process of age assessment in immigration cases. Age-disputed individuals should not be detained unless and until a professional age assessment has been undertaken by the panel. Although the role of this body could be limited to age assessment, given the other safeguards that need to be put in place to protect those children who are detained, its remit could be broader than this. This extended remit is discussed in Section Four.

In addition, and regardless of which route is followed, the important issue of where these age-disputed individuals should be accommodated while the age assessment is carried out will also need to be addressed. The reality is that IND caseworkers can and do wrongly assess children to be over the age of 18. Because the risks of detaining a potential child are so high, it is clearly not appropriate to detain age-disputed individuals while their age assessment is undertaken. Age assessments require time and other resources.

One option is to provide those whose age is disputed with group accommodation through a local authority provider. Some of those with whom we discussed this option raised concerns about the possible risks to some children if a proportion of those who are housed with them are subsequently assessed as being adults. While this may not be ideal, it remains a lower risk than detaining possible children with known adults in a stressful environment which they are unable to leave if they are subject to, or fear, abuse. It is also no higher risk than the accommodation provided by many social services to children aged 16 and 17 (and sometimes as

young as 15) in unsupervised bed and breakfast accommodation. We understand that such an approach to age assessment has already been piloted by the Home Office in Dover, with age-disputed individuals being given Temporary Admission for seven days and housed while an assessment of their age is made. Although the University of Kent in Canterbury is currently carrying out research on the effectiveness of this approach, no further information was available at the time of writing.

3.4.3 Guardianship

Although the focus of this section has been on the process of age assessment, it is important to recognise that separated children have a whole range of needs that go beyond the issue of detention and asylum determination. For this reason and to ensure that their needs and experiences are taken into account across all the different areas of policy and practice, the Separated Children in Europe Programme (SCEP) believes that every child should have a guardian (SCEP 2004). At an ideas exchange on guardianship for separated children in the UK held in June 2004 and organised by Save the Children, UNHCR, and Refugee Council as part of the SCEP, there was a consensus that the present system of support does not adequately safeguard the best interests of all separated children and that there is a need for a coherent system of guardianship. This need is not limited to separated children who are seeking asylum but may extend to other separated children. The role of the guardian would primarily be to identify and prioritise the best interests of the separated child.

Key findings

- Children are currently detained in the UK as part of fast track procedures for asylum determination. The purpose of the fast track procedures is primarily administrative convenience. These children are not subject to Removal Directions at the time that the decision to detain is made and there is rarely any evidence to suggest that they would not comply with the conditions of Temporary Admission if they were not detained.

- Processes for ensuring that there are no obstacles to removal and that the welfare of children is taken into account in the decision to detain are not always effective. This increases the risk that children will be detained unnecessarily or without any imminent prospect for their removal. Case reviews are a key mechanism for safeguarding against the inappropriate or unlawful detention of children.

- Social service age assessments are not routinely undertaken. Where formal age assessments are undertaken, these may be based on different criteria. The Home Office does not always take social service age assessments into account, contrary to stated policy. An entirely different approach to age assessment is required in order to avoid the additional risks associated with the detention of separated children.

Recommendations

- Children should not be detained as part of fast track procedures for asylum determination.

- The most effective way of ensuring that the decision to detain children is fully informed is to ensure that those with ultimate responsibility for the decision to detain – enforcement officers working on the ground – are able to access the family's case file at first hand.

- A pastoral visit should be always be undertaken prior to a decision to detain. The aim of this visit should be to ensure that all the factors relevant to the decision to detain are taken into account. This visit should also be used as an opportunity to put in place alternative mechanisms for ensuring compliance which avoid the need to detain children.

- No decision to detain should be made unless and until a formal age assessment has been undertaken by social services. Better still, an independent age assessment dispute panel should be established, comprised of independent social workers, experienced paediatricians and other relevant professionals. The establishment of the panel should be undertaken with the consensus and support of statutory and voluntary organisations in order to ensure that only one set of criteria is used for the process of age assessment in immigration cases. Age-disputed individuals should not be detained unless and until there is a formal age assessment undertaken by the panel.

Notes

36 See http://www.iaa.gov.uk/appendix_1_IS_operation_enforcement_manual_chapter_38.pdf

37 The revised family removal instructions are as yet unpublished but after some delay will be included as a specific chapter in the OEM, which is due to be published early in 2005.

38 The policy of giving age-disputed individuals the benefit of the doubt in 'borderline' cases is set out in the OEM. According to stated Home Office policy, fast track procedures such as those at Oakington are also unsuitable for unaccompanied children and age-dispute cases "other than those where their appearance *strongly* suggests that they are over 18 years" (emphasis in original).

39 *Screening Best Practice for Operational Staff (At Ports)* (Version 210803), available at www.jcwi.org.uk/lawpolicy/uklaw/screeninguide.pdf

40 *R (on the application of B) v London Borough of Merton* [2003] EWHC 1689

41 *C v The London Borough of Enfield* [2004] EWHC 2297

42 *Berhe v London Borough of Hillingdon* [2003] EWHC 2075 (Admin). For further information see www.childrenslegalcentre.com/shared_asp_files/uploadedfiles/{41A E5280-392F-4692-90CB-D28F77E56CD7}_Care%20and%20support.pdf

43 *R (on the application of A) v SSHD* [2004] CO/2858/2004

4 Alternatives to the detention of children

In the UK there is a presumption in favour of temporary release or admission and the Home Office has stated that that, wherever possible, IND will use alternatives to detention (Home Office 1998, 2001). However, the evidence collected during the course of our research indicates while there is a whole range of alternatives available to policy-makers in order to maintain contact, ensure compliance and even secure the departure of asylum-seekers whose applications have been refused, that these are not used in a systematic or coherent way. Despite the fact that detention is both financially and emotionally costly and politically contentious, it continues to be treated as a low-risk strategy for securing compliance.

Alternatives to detention are meaningful only if they exist within a broader system of decision-making that ensures ongoing and consistent contact is maintained, and where asylum-seekers have information about their rights and are aware of their obligations. Reflecting this overall approach to alternatives, this section explores a range of mechanisms for delivering information and maintaining contact with families that increase compliance and reduce the perceived need to detain families with children in order to maintain the integrity of UK immigration controls. These are:
* reporting
* electronic monitoring
* supervised accommodation
* community supervision
* incentivised compliance.

Issues of separating children from their families and voluntary return are also examined in this section.

4.1 What do we mean by 'alternatives'?

One important obstacle to the use of alternatives in the UK appears to be the lack of mutual understanding about what is meant by 'alternatives'. IND is keen to point out that most children who are subject to immigration control are not detained and that detention only takes place when it is not otherwise possible to ensure compliance with procedures, particularly where these relate to removal. Our concern is that this situation – and the perception that there is no alternative other than to detain a family – arises in significant part because of inadequate and inconsistent contact and information between asylum applicants and the Home Office prior to this point.

Our approach to the concept of alternatives is therefore one that focuses less on control and more on the maintenance of contact and compliance through mechanisms that provide support and information, and enhance the quality and credibility of the asylum determination process overall. There is no evidence that more control is needed to ensure compliance on the part of asylum-seekers – including families. Therefore possible alternatives to the detention of children must be considered strictly in those terms. Moreover, any restrictions to freedom of choice or movement employed as an alternative to detention must be justified. The fact that any particular alternative is less negative than detention does not imply that it may be applied arbitrarily. Restrictions on liberty imposed as alternatives to detention must still comply with international standards.

The alternatives which we present here relate primarily to children in families. The issues around the detention of children whose age is disputed are rather different. The Government has at no stage implied that it is necessary or justified to detain unaccompanied children other than overnight and for their own safety. As such, there is by corollary no need to seek alternatives to detention. Rather, the priority is to ensure that an individual whose age is disputed is not detained unless and until there has been a professional assessment of his or her age as recommended in the previous section.

Our detailed discussion of bail as a mechanism for ensuring that where a decision to detain children is taken this detention does not become prolonged can be found in Section Five. However, it should be noted here that there is some evidence in relation to bail to support our conclusion that – in contrast to what is often assumed – asylum-seekers are generally willing to comply with immigration procedures controls. Research by Bruegel and Natamba (2002) indicates that the majority of those detained and released on bail comply with their bail conditions. Ninety-eight asylum detainees bailed between July 2000 and October 2001 were traced through to the winter of 2001/2002. Ninety per cent of those bailed were found to have kept to their bail conditions, and of these 7 per cent were granted leave to remain or refugee status by the end of the project. This high compliance rate has included compliance with removal directions. Fifteen per cent of those tracked were bailed awaiting removal, and of these 80 per cent complied with bail restrictions and were successfully removed. These conclusions are supported by other research. A survey of 185 bail applications presented to the IAA between 2000 and 2003 found that 79 per cent of those on bail complied with bail terms (Ionel, McClean and Mobbs 2003). The authors emphasise that these compliance figures relate to those who had been considered by IND to be at high risk of absconding. They conclude that even in these cases, detention was not in fact necessary to ensure compliance.

4.2 International standards and guidelines

States, keeping in mind that detention should be a measure of last resort and for the shortest period of time and in light of the best interests of the child

principle, should provide appropriate alternatives to the detention of children, exploring in full the options of reporting obligations, guarantor requirements, supervised group accommodation or quality extra-familial care services through fostering or residential care arrangements . . . States should consider all appropriate alternatives to detention in the case of children accompanying their parents and detention, in such cases, should be considered only if it is the sole means of maintaining family unity. (UNHCR 2002: 8)

UNHCR (1999, 2002) has set out a range of alternatives that should be used in preference to detaining children. Detention should only take place after a full consideration of all possible alternatives, or when monitoring mechanisms have been demonstrated not to be effective. Where there are monitoring mechanisms that can be employed as viable alternatives to detention, these should be applied *first* unless there is evidence to suggest that such an alternative will not be effective in the individual case. The UNHCR's (1999) detention guidelines set out a number of alternatives to detention including monitoring through reporting or residency requirements, provision of a guarantor or surety, release on bail or the use of open centres.

Restrictions on liberty imposed as alternatives to detention must still comply with international standards on the restriction of liberty. The UN Standard Minimum Rules for Non-Custodial Measures (the 'Tokyo Rules') set out the principles relating to non-custodial sentencing in the criminal justice field and are most analogous to alternatives available in the immigration context (ECRE 1997). The Tokyo Rules require that supervision should not be carried out in a way that would harass individuals, jeopardise their dignity or intrude on their privacy or that of their families. Methods of supervision that treat asylum-seekers solely as objects of control should not be employed. Surveillance techniques should not be used without the asylum-seekers' knowledge. Supervision should be periodically reviewed and adjusted as necessary. Moreover the failure of a non-custodial measure should not automatically lead to the imposition of a custodial measure.

4.3 Separating children from their parents

Before moving on to our analysis of the various mechanisms that are available to policy-makers to deliver increased contact, it is important to consider briefly whether separating children from their parents is an appropriate alternative to detention in those cases where IND considers detention to be the only way to secure compliance.

The separation of children from their parents is a difficult and controversial issue and one that is never far beneath the surface in discussions about the detention of children in the immigration context. As a matter of policy, IND aims to keep the family as a single unit except in those cases where it is appropriate to separate a child from his or her parents if there is evidence that separation is in the best interests of the child. This policy of non-separation extends to fast track procedures, although the Home Office has left open the option of separating dependants from a claimant on those occasions "when we believe it necessary and right to do so".[44] The circumstances under which children would be separated from their parents or carers for fast track procedures are not specified.

It is important to acknowledge that the separation of children from one of their parents is a mechanism for securing compliance that is already utilised by IND. In one of our case studies, Precious and her baby Martine, aged six months, were detained but the baby's father was not. In the case of Sofia, Visar and Michael, described in detail earlier in this report, only the father was detained on the first occasion, at his request. In another case, two children aged four years and 20 months were detained with their mother and their father only discovered this at a later date. In another three cases, there is evidence suggesting that initially the parents were detained without their children and that their children joined them at a later stage. In the last of these cases, Shontelle was detained for around 60 days before being joined by her eight-year-old daughter. She also had three other children under 15, who were cared for by grown-up children.

Finally, and of most concern, is the case of Esma and Dermo and their daughters Nina (aged seven) and Sibel (aged five). Their experiences are discussed in more detail in Section Five. The family was detained for around a month before Esma was sectioned under the Mental Health Act and taken to hospital. She was five months pregnant. When she was returned to Dungavel she experienced a miscarriage and was again sectioned and taken to hospital. While she was in hospital the children were released on Temporary Admission with their father and eventually returned to London so they could go back to school. Although independent medical reports indicated that Esma was suicidal and needed to be with her children, they were separated from her for a further three months and unable to visit her because she was so far away.

It is difficult to know whether the negative impact on children of being separated from parents or carers is better or worse than the negative impact of detention. Counter-posing these as 'choices' does not seem appropriate. Moreover, in cases involving one-parent families this is not an option, leading to the conclusion that children in this situation are perhaps more likely to find themselves being detained than children where two parents are 'available' for detention. Nonetheless, one stakeholder whom we interviewed suggested that this 'choice' ought at least to be considered:

> By accepting the 'never separate argument', we are failing to look at the interests of the child. Children shouldn't be treated as adjuncts of their parents but rather as having their own interests and rights. If you take seriously the impact of detention on children, you must consider what is worse, detention or separation from parent?

For the most part, there is a consensus that removing a child from their parent or parents is excessively penalising and traumatic for both children and parents. However, this must be balanced against penalising children for the Home Office's view of their parents' risk of absconding, and against the impact of detention. In Sweden, if a family's identity cannot be ascertained or there is a question of threat to national security, one parent is held in detention, while the other parent and children are released into a group home. There is access to regular visitation and telephone contact. These cases are given first priority so as to ensure that the family is reunited as quickly as possible (Mitchell 2001). Agencies in Sweden have reported that, in most cases, parents who are given a choice opt to split the family rather than have their child or children remain in detention. In cases where there is only a father and child, and for extreme reasons the father will not be released, the child will normally be released into a group home for unaccompanied children with regular access to the father (Field, forthcoming). This approach must be understood in the context of very different provision for the support of asylum-seekers, less use of detention generally and statutory time limits on detention itself.

Within our case studies, we did find some evidence that parents would prefer to be separated from their children than for their children to be detained with them. For example, Shontelle told us that she preferred being separated from three other children to having them with them with her in Dungavel, especially given the impacts of detention on her youngest daughter, Leah. However, this was only because she had grown-up children already in the UK who she felt confident would be able to care for them appropriately. It was clear from comments made by other parents that if they were going to be detained they would prefer to have their children with them, not least because of anxieties about the future and the fear of being removed from the UK without them and therefore becoming permanently separated.

This evidence suggests that the decision about whether or not it would be appropriate to separate a child from his or her parents or carers will very much depend upon the particular circumstances of the case and what is judged to be in the child's best interests. In such cases it seems appropriate that parents, and where possible their children, should be part of this decision-making process. The problem is that this kind of case-by-case assessment of the best interests of any particular child does not currently appear to be undertaken and there does not appear to be any mechanism for making it happen. Moreover, it assumes that there are no alternatives available to the

decision to detain in the first place. As one stakeholder commented:

We can't counter-pose the two to justify incarcerating children. The alternative is to let families out and put them in places where children can come and go.

The evidence presented in the following section suggests that there are a number of alternatives available to policy-makers that increase compliance without separating children from their parents.

4.4 Contact and information – an alternative approach to compliance

The evidence collected during the course of this research suggests that IND consider it necessary to detain some children in families in order to speed up asylum processing, prevent applicants from absconding and ensure compliance with removal at the end of the decision-making process. Given this context, our analysis focuses on those mechanisms that are known to improve the level of contact and co-operation between the Home Office and asylum applicants, including families with children. During the course of our research, the issue of information provision emerged as a particularly significant factor in ensuring that a greater range of alternatives to the detention of children are made available and can be used to the benefit of both children and the decision-making process as a whole.

There is currently a limited and inconsistent flow of information between the decision-maker and the applicant during the period when a decision is being made about the application for asylum. As a result, applicants may not be fully aware of their obligations, they may feel insecure or uncertain about the process and its outcome and fail to attend interviews or other significant meetings, they or their children may be ill or otherwise unable to fulfill reporting requirements, or they may be unaware of the options available to them, including the possibility of being supported to return to the country of origin where appropriate. All of these factors may influence the applicant's ability or willingness to comply with the asylum process.

The Home Office meanwhile may effectively lose contact with the applicant for a whole range of reasons. These can include, for example, inadequate sharing of information within and between departments, including information about changes of address and legal representatives, or the failure of the legal representative – where there is one – to keep IND informed about changes in the family's circumstances which may be relevant in any decision. In addition, the current culture of decision-making within IND can lead to actions being taken at pre-determined points in the process, regardless of whether these are effective in minimising the detention of children and ensuring that any detention that does occur does not become prolonged.

Poor information flows between an applicant and the Home Office mean that confidence in the decision-making process is low. When a decision is reached and an attempt made to remove a family, it may be assumed that they are not willing to comply with Removal Directions because new issues are brought to light at this stage or because contact has been lost altogether. This is clearly an unsatisfactory situation for both the applicant and the Home Office. Our evidence indicates that it can result in the detention of children that is neither appropriate nor necessary and that it undermines the quality of the decision-making process overall, leading to additional financial and other costs.

Our research has also found that improved information flows can improve contact between asylum-seekers and the decision-making authorities, so that the decision to detain is truly a measure of last resort. The importance of information provision, and the trust it can help create, runs in parallel to views that a credible determination system instils greater compliance tendencies. Immigration officers have expressed the view that quick and credible determination procedures acted as an encouragement to voluntary compliance with Removal Directions (Weber and Gelsthorpe 2000). Evidence from Sweden suggests that detention can be avoided altogether in

many cases since people are more likely to comply even with final decisions if they are prepared and empowered throughout the determination process (Justice for Asylum-seekers Alliance 2002).

In countries such as Sweden this is achieved through a system in which each asylum applicant is assigned a caseworker with responsibility for maintaining contact with the family and providing information about the decision-making process and its outcomes. Detention may be imposed at any time in the application process for asylum-seekers if it is determined that they arrived on false documentation, but this will occur only after consultation with the applicant's caseworker, who will also consider the alternative option of imposing reporting requirements once to three times a week (Mitchell 2001).

Both the Swedish system and the Appearance Assistance Program (AAP) piloted by the Vera Institute in the United States (discussed in detail below) have a strong focus on informing people of the system and processes, their options, and reasons for measures taken. In both cases, information is provided in person by a caseworker, rather than in generic forms. In the UK there is also some evidence that information services – particularly legal advice and support – are important in encouraging people to maintain contact and comply with regulations (Cole 2003).

4.5 Mechanisms for delivering contact and information

Mechanisms for delivering contact and information that create alternatives to the detention of children exist both in the UK and internationally. Few of these alternatives are mutually exclusive. Accommodation-based alternatives, for example, often have reporting requirements built into them. Community release programmes are frequently linked to bail and sureties structures. The only alternative that can be wholly independent is reporting, although the most effective reporting systems also include incentives, notably the provision of information, access to services and individual relationships with caseworkers.

Given existing evidence about the importance of two-way information flows between asylum applicants and the authorities for improving decision-making and ensuring compliance, this section of our report examines the specific options for delivering improvements in this area. What these approaches have in common is the objective of increasing contact between asylum applicants and the authorities. They vary significantly, however, in the extent to which this is a two-way process which also provides support and information to the applicant. Approaches that provide most support and information are, in our view, most likely to open up genuine alternatives to the detention of children and to have beneficial impacts on the asylum determination process more generally.

4.5.1 Reporting

Reporting is the most widely used alternative to detention and requires asylum-seekers to attend a designated location on a regular basis. Reporting requirements are generally imposed when individuals are granted Temporary Admission or after release on bail. The purpose of reporting is to ensure that there is regular contact between those subject to immigration control and the authorities. Because reporting is the simplest and least intrusive of all alternatives to detention other than unconditional liberty, it is the mechanism for maintaining contact used in a number of countries. In France for example, there is no official reporting system, but in effect this is the main control mechanism. Asylum-seekers and others subject to immigration control need to renew their 'authorisation de séjour' papers every three months, and also need to collect financial assistance every month, which requires a fixed address. In addition, those who fall under Schengen agreements need to renew their Schengen stamp once a fortnight (ECRE 1997). In effect, this means applicants must report to the authorities between once every ten days to once every three weeks or so.

It is important to recognise that the use of reporting as a mechanism for maintaining contact is not without its problems. Reporting mechanisms in the UK are currently not user-friendly. Factors that can affect their effectiveness are primarily related to the frequency of required reporting and the distance from where the

person lives. Requirements may be as demanding as having to report several times a week or even daily, at a particular time of day, perhaps some distance from home. This increases the risk that applicants will miss their slot and be deemed to have failed to report (ILPA and BID 2003). Alternatively, requirements may be limited to having to report at any time of day on a regular day once a month.

The frequency of reporting requirements also needs to be considered in conjunction with the fact that asylum-seekers have very limited income, and those deemed to have reached the end of the process possibly have no recourse to funds at all. There is some evidence that the recent emphasis on the use of Immigration Service Reporting Centres rather than local police stations has resulted in longer travelling times, as there are fewer reporting centres than police stations (ILPA and BID 2003). In April 2002, seven reporting centres were set up in the UK, with asylum-seekers within a 25-mile or 90-minute traveling radius having to report to one of them (Human Rights First 2002).

Evidence from our case study sample confirms that while reporting is preferable to the detention of children, it is not without its difficulties where it is used as a blunt control mechanism. Leah's mother, Shontelle, told us that reporting arrangements cause her practical and financial difficulties:

> *I am reporting every week. It is half an hour or 45 minutes by bus. I go alone. Sometimes I don't have money for the bus fare to report and I ask for help. I want to work but I'm not allowed. What we have, we get from family.*

Marcia told us that she did not find it too difficult to report when Sylvie and John are in school but that it is more difficult if they are ill or on holiday:

> *I have to report every week. It takes about one hour each way. I go when the children are in school. Now they're on holidays. I haven't missed a signing.*

For one of the families in our case study sample, contact with the Home Office appears to have been lost when the family was rehoused by NASS in a different area of the UK.

4.5.2 Age-disputed cases and reporting

It is also important to recognise that different issues arise in relation to reporting for children whose age is disputed. These children can find it difficult to remember and plan for appointments and may be at particular risk of being detained on the assumption that they have stopped reporting because they have absconded. Bem, who was detained when he was 16 years old, told us that although he does not report directly to IND he often forgets to sign in with social services:

I don't have to report. I have to sign here in this house, it's part of the rules. Most times I forget. I have a doctor, and a social worker, and I go to college.

We also found some evidence that even where legitimate reasons for failing to report are provided, these do not necessarily reach the right person or are taken into account when the decision is made to detain. This can have dramatic consequences. Jacques, the 17-year-old boy whose experiences were described in detail in Section Two, told us that he had been detained after he had failed to report but that he had informed his social worker that he had flu and that she had in turn contacted the reporting centre and advised them of this. It appears that there had been a

Emmanuel, Solange and Thomas (aged 13 months)

Emmanuel arrived in the UK in 2000, and claimed asylum within three days. His wife Solange followed two years later, and claimed asylum on the day she arrived. Both Emmanuel's and Solange's asylum claims were refused, and their appeals in early 2002 were dismissed. By early 2003, both appeals to the Tribunal had been rejected. Emmanuel submitted a fresh asylum and human rights claim. This application was refused a couple of months later.

During their time in the UK, the couple were required to report once a month and did so. The couple moved, apparently in a NASS-arranged move. Their son, Thomas, was born shortly afterwards. The family informed NASS that they had been required to report when in London. NASS reportedly said that they would send a fax to the Immigration Service to inform them of the move.

Between March and August 2003, Emmanuel did not report, though Solange did. After this time both Emmanuel and Solange reported once a week as required. Despite complying with reporting requirements, the family were detained in the summer of 2004 and taken to Dungavel. An attempt was made to remove them shortly afterwards but this was resisted. After a further failed removal attempt, the family was transferred to Oakington.

Shortly afterwards, BID represented the couple at a bail hearing. The family's bail summaries acknowledged that neither of them had ever absconded, but that the family received a pastoral visit prior to their detention during which they stated that they did not want to return to their country of origin. This was used as an indication that it would not be possible to remove the family from the UK without the use of detention. The couple had no sureties, and could not provide a bail address as they had been in NASS accommodation. NASS stated it could not provide accommodation to those who were resisting removal. Bail was refused and the family was subsequently removed from the UK. They had been detained for a total of 61 days.

breakdown in communication and the Home Office did not record this information.

4.5.3 More effective use of reporting

The issues raised in our case studies suggest that the problem with the current approach to the use of reporting as an alternative to detention is that it is used principally as a mechanism for controlling the whereabouts of asylum-seekers rather than as a co-operative, two-way process for maintaining contact. If things go wrong, for whatever reason, there is an assumption that the family or age-disputed individual has deliberately lost contact or failed to comply. Efforts to re-establish contact may not be made unless and until there is a further development in the case, most notably a negative decision or Removal Direction, which requires some kind of action to be taken to re-establish contact and compliance. At this stage an assessment is made about whether detention is necessary, based on an immigration history that records that non-compliance has occurred in the past. Consequently, but possibly erroneously, detention becomes viewed as an appropriate measure.

If there is a genuine desire to identify alternatives to detention that are cost-effective and enable better contact to be maintained without the negative impacts associated with detention, then reporting mechanisms need to be developed that view the arrangement as a mutually beneficial one for both the applicant and the Home Office. At a basic level, this would require flexibility in the way in which reporting requirements are currently imposed, including ensuring a child-friendly reporting system that recognises families' childcare needs, such as taking children to school or travel logistics for parents with babies; allowing flexibility in the times people have to report; or acceding to requests that, for example, reporting need not be on a day of the week when individuals have other significant commitments. It would also require a recognition that because age-disputed individuals are sometimes children, requiring them to report at particular times is not realistic unless there is a responsible adult ensuring they attend. For all asylum-seekers, the Home Office should meet costs associated with reporting so that this does not undermine its effectiveness as a mechanism for maintaining contact.

It is our understanding that the Home Office has begun to recognise the need for a graded scale to apply reporting requirements more appropriately, and that there is a need to make it is easier for asylum-seekers to report, for example through increasing the number of reporting centres and introducing mobile reporting centres. It is important to acknowledge, however, that the current model for reporting, even if significantly improved, does not provide information to asylum-seekers about their rights, obligations or the options that may be available to them. Creating significant workable alternatives to the detention of children will require the development of a reporting system that incorporates support, information and meaningful contact.

4.5.4 Electronic monitoring

The use of electronic monitoring in its various forms to maintain better contact with those subject to immigration control is an issue that has been the subject of intense debate in the UK over recent months. Increased monitoring of asylum-seekers was announced in a White Paper in 2002 and the introduction of Asylum Registration Cards, in conjunction with increasing use of reporting requirements, is consistent with this objective.[45] Section 36 of the Asylum and Immigration (Treatment of Claimants, etc) Act (2004) creates provision for the electronic monitoring of those over the age of 18 who are subject to immigration control. This will consist of several different elements:

- the use of voice recognition technology which will in some cases negate the need to report to an immigration reporting centre or police station in person
- the use of other forms of electronic monitoring (tagging and tracking) as an alternative to detention "for those at the lower end of the risk spectrum, or for those who in the absence of suitable sureties would otherwise have remained in detention."

There are concerns about the implications of these measures for the civil liberties of asylum-seekers who have committed no crime and would not otherwise be detained because they are not considered to be at risk of absconding. The concern is that, in relation to tagging and tracking at least, the technology will be used in addition to – rather than instead of – detention, resulting in greater control over asylum-seekers but not necessarily improvements in communication nor a reduction in detention. It is not clear whether those who are already detained will be released if they agree to be monitored electronically or whether this monitoring will instead be imposed on those who would not otherwise have been detained. The extent to which electronic monitoring represents an alternative rather than an additional measure to detention will reflect how it is used in practice and which approach prevails.

Electronic monitoring of asylum-seekers has taken place in the United States since 2003. In Miami, Florida, a programme initiated by the Department of Homeland Security, involves tagging devices being fitted on to asylum-seekers released from detention. Two significant problems have been identified with the programme. The first concerns the disproportionate use of electronic monitoring in cases where release on parole may be adequate. This was linked to concern that the devices were not being used to minimise the use of detention, but rather to impose more intrusive conditions on released individuals than existed prior to the programme. The second problem concerns the conditions of the programme. Tagged asylum-seekers are not permitted to leave their homes for more than five hours, and this hampers their ability to meet their lawyers or attend to medical or family matters. The Miami electronic monitoring device programme is now being implemented nationwide.

A programme largely based on the Appearance Assistance Program pilot is being rolled out this year, for 200 individuals in each of eight cities in the United States. Unlike the AAP, the Intensive Supervision Program (ISAP) includes the use of electronic tagging. The participants will include asylum-seekers but also 'criminal aliens' and 'aliens on order of supervision'. As with the Miami programme, concern has been expressed that the ISAP may be applied to immigrants who would otherwise be released from detention without supervision, instead of to detainees who would not otherwise be released (Human Rights First 2004).

Given that there is no research to show how many people abscond, there is no evidential basis for introducing the policy of tagging. As a result, it is difficult to determine whether this approach has the potential to reduce the use of detention by enabling better contact to be maintained. Moreover, because the provision to order electronic monitoring is not restrained by any criteria, appeal or time limit and there is no burden on the state to demonstrate that it is a necessary or appropriate measure for a particular individual, its use may not comply with the provisions of the Tokyo Rules, outlined earlier in this section. It has also been suggested to us that such a policy is inherently contradictory. As with all electronic arrangements – including those used in the criminal justice system – tagging is reliant upon the co-operation and compliance of the person who is being monitored. This is recognised by the Home Office.[46] Without this consent the tag can simply be removed. This would appear to make the system superfluous: if asylum-seekers must co-operate with electronic monitoring in order for it to function, it is not clear why the system is needed at all since a willingness to comply with immigration controls has already been demonstrated.

Most importantly perhaps for the purpose of our analysis, the various forms of electronic monitoring which are being considered and piloted fail to meet the most important objective for ensuring compliance, namely the provision of meaningful two-way contact combined with support and information. Indeed, it is difficult to conceive of a less meaningful relationship between the Home Office and applicants. Such an approach also represents a misguided reliance upon technology to deliver solutions when we know that it can, and does, go wrong and that it is inherently inflexible in responding to changes in an individual's circumstances.

With the exception of voice recognition-based reporting which, if used with these caveats in mind, has the potential to improve the ease of maintaining contact with the Home Office, all the available evidence suggests that there are better, more effective and less expensive alternatives to detention than electronic tagging and tracking. If additional resources are to be found to enhance contact between asylum-seekers and the Home Office and reduce the need for detention, then these should be directed towards an alternative model for providing information and meaningful contact and ensuring that quality legal advice and representation is available throughout the determination process. This adds far greater value to the asylum determination process as a whole than simply investing resources in technologies to increase control.

4.5.5 Supervised accommodation

One mechanism for providing contact and information is to accommodate asylum-seekers while their application for asylum is being determined and to ensure that meaningful contact and information, including legal advice and representation, is available *in situ*. Maintaining contact through supervised accommodation can take different forms. These range from large accommodation centres in isolated areas that do not differ significantly from reception or removal centres, to 'clusters' of private flats such as those used in Sweden, through to a simple and verifiable requirement to live at a designated address.

The use of supervised accommodation as an appropriate and less damaging alternative to the detention of children is dependent upon the form that this accommodation takes and the restrictions that it entails. In Germany, Switzerland and the Netherlands, residence in a collective centre is compulsory for part or all of the asylum procedure. NGOs, social workers and medical practitioners have reported problems with compulsory collective accommodation, including depression and a loss of independence. Open centres can provide an alternative in cases where asylum-seekers might otherwise be held in detention, as such centres can control the whereabouts of the residents to varying degrees. In Belgium, Norway, Denmark, Slovakia, Poland and the Czech Republic, eligibility for financial assistance is conditional upon residence in such a centre (ECRE 1997). In some open centres, the authorities operate a curfew at night but allow the residents to leave during the day. In others, residents are asked to register whenever they leave and re-enter the centre, stating where they intend to go during each excursion. In many cases, however, these centres are

situated in inconveniently remote locations, and this in itself serves as a form of control on the residents' movements.

In Sweden by contrast, families and separated children are not considered to require close supervision, and children, including those who arrive without documentation, are not routinely detained. Instead, they are accommodated in the Carlslun reception centre where their health and support needs are assessed. Within two weeks they are released to regional refugee centres. These are made up of groups of flats in small communities close to the central office reception. A caseworker is assigned to each asylum-seeker on arrival. This caseworker explains the refugee determination process and an asylum-seeker's rights during the time they are awaiting a decision. The caseworker also ensures that asylum applications are processed correctly and that legal representation and interpreters are provided if necessary (Mitchell 2001). Residents are required to visit the reception office caseworkers at least once a month, to receive their allowance, news on their application, and a monthly need and risk assessment. Referrals to counselling and medical care are also provided by caseworkers. During their time at the reception centre, all residents are free to move around with minimal supervision. Living in the group flats is not a requirement, though registering and staying in touch with the reception office is. This level of combined monitoring and support has proved beneficial to both asylum-seekers and the authorities. Applicants have been more willing to comply with asylum decisions, even when these end with a deportation order (ECRE 1997).

In 2001 the Home Office announced that four accommodation centres housing 3,000 asylum applicants would be opened on a trial basis in 2002. The development of the centres has been delayed due largely to local opposition, but there is evidence that the Government still intends to pursue this approach. The centres are planned in non-urban areas, with health, education and legal services provided within the centre rather than locally. 'Residents' will be able to come and go from the centres but will be required to live there, and there will be reporting requirements to demonstrate their ongoing residency. It should be noted, however, that the Home Office's intention that people considered at risk of absconding will not be placed in accommodation centres, suggests that this supervised accommodation is not designed to provide an alternative to detention, but rather increased restrictions for people who would not otherwise be detained. This is of particular concern, given that the conditions of the proposed accommodation centres do not differ markedly from removal centres. The impacts on children who are held there will therefore not be significantly different from those described earlier in this report. Moreover, we have not seen any evidence that a caseworker approach similar to that developed in Sweden would be adopted. In the absence of dedicated caseworkers working with individuals and families, the proposed accommodation centres will add limited value to the existing approach.

4.5.6 Community supervision

Community supervision is effectively a mechanism for establishing a relationship between asylum applicants and the community in which they are resident, through which information and support can be channelled, and contact with the authorities more effectively maintained. Community supervision has been successfully piloted in Australia and the United States. The Hotham Mission in Melbourne, for example, has shown how community or church-based agencies are able to provide comprehensive support to asylum-seekers, while also optimising compliance (Justice for Asylum-seekers Alliance 2002). Mission workers have taken on caseworker roles in empowering clients to make the few decisions they can and advocating for them between service providers and the Australian Department of Immigration and Multicultural Affairs (ADIMA). Their experience indicates that the provision of adequate legal representation to asylum-seekers, combined with an awareness of the immigration process, means they are more likely to feel they have had a fair hearing. In addition, the provision of further support, such as following-up on return or organising for the Red Cross to meet them, greatly assists an asylum-seeker whose application is refused to make the difficult journey home, and allows for third country options to be explored on a final negative decision.

The Hotham Mission reports extremely high figures in clients' compliance with decisions. These benefits were most obvious with clients who had been in contact with the Hotham Mission from the earliest stages of their asylum applications. The Mission concluded this was a clear endorsement of consistent and ongoing case management of asylum-seekers both in detention and in the community (Justice for Asylum-seekers Alliance 2002).

These conclusions are similar to those drawn from a project co-ordinated by the Lutheran Immigration and Refugee Service in the United States. As part of this project, the immigration authorities released 25 Chinese asylum-seekers from detention in Illinois to shelters in several communities. The community shelters took on the role of reminding participants of their hearings, scheduling check-ins with the INS, organising transport and accompanying asylum-seekers to their appointments. Non-profit agencies also found pro bono attorneys for all the asylum-seekers who were released to the shelters. The project achieved a 96 per cent appearance rate (Human Rights First 2004).

Other US projects include Gay Hartner's Refugee Immigration Ministry in Boston, supported by a local congregation. Vermont Refugee Assistance, which began in 1987, is a similar local approach through which volunteers organise 'host homes' for asylum-seekers so that they can be released to an individual citizen's responsibility. The People of the Golden Vision (an NGO set up in Pennsylvania to help the Chinese who landed on the Golden Venture boat in 1993) purchased a 'halfway house' to accommodate asylum-seekers whom the authorities would otherwise insist on detaining (ECRE 1997).

These examples suggest that community supervision can be an extremely effective alternative to detention because it ensures compliance with determination procedures up to the point at which a final decision is made. What is not clear from this evidence is whether such compliance would also be secured at the end of the process when all the options for remaining in the UK have been exhausted: in other words, at the point where the Home Office often maintains that there is no alternative other than to detain a family in order to ensure compliance with Removal Directions. It is currently assumed by the Home Office that it would not. This conclusion is drawn from the response of the Home Office to a proposal made by the Refuge Scotland Group (chaired by Michael Connarty MP) to establish a pilot project called Asylum-seekers Housing Support (ASHS) which would house families being detained at the Dungavel Removal Centre near Glasgow. The proposed pilot, which was supported by a wide range of churches and charities, was to provide accommodation for up to nine families within self-contained flats, and to offer practical support, facilities, counselling and advocacy services for them. The proposal thus encompassed elements of supervised accommodation and community release.

The proposal was rejected by the Home Office on the basis that the issue for these families was not one of providing accommodation (which was already being provided by NASS prior to detention in most cases) but of ensuring the family did not abscond before they could be removed from the UK. The difficulty with the model proposed by the ASHS was as much related to the context in which it was located as its content. Because a judgement had already been made by the IND about the families concerned, the alternative effectively came too late in the decision-making process. In our view, there remains scope to consider such an approach, provided that this accommodation and the system of support and information is made available during the decision-making process itself (ideally at its outset) and *prior* to the decision to detain.

4.5.7 Incentivised compliance

The mechanisms for delivering contact and information which have been presented thus far fulfil our requirements for an alternative approach to the detention of children to varying degrees. Reporting and electronic monitoring enable contact to be improved but deliver little if anything in terms of meaningful contact or two-way provision of information between the Home Office and asylum applicants. Supervised accommodation can, if based on a caseworker approach, meet this objective. However, where it is pursued primarily as a mechanism for maintaining contact rather than

delivering improvements to the asylum process as a whole, it can result in conditions that replicate those experienced by children in removal centres and therefore fail to provide a genuine alternative. Community supervision has the potential to offer a meaningful alternative, but only if it is available from the beginning of the decision-making process.

Reflecting the limitations of these alternatives, we propose the development of a reporting system that incorporates support, information and meaningful contact. This system should be based on existing evidence about what works and the elements that are needed to ensure an effective and workable alternative to the detention of children.

The Appearance Assistance Program (AAP) that was piloted in the United States by the Vera Institute on behalf of the immigration authorities exemplifies such a system. This programme, which operated in New York for three years until 2000, could be categorised as a reporting system but it is much more comprehensive, and its resources more eclectic. Furthermore, the elements of the programme that set it aside from crude reporting schemes can be found in some of the other alternatives that were discussed above. These elements include one-to-one caseworker relationships, with an emphasis on mutual trust, assistance with accessing services – particularly legal advice and representation – and the provision of general and specific information on the asylum process and the progress of participants' cases.

Possible participants in the AAP were selected from new arrivals as well as detainees recommended by detention centre staff. All of those who took part in the pilot were people who were either detained or whom the immigration authorities indicated would be detained were it not for the project's alternative. Suitability for participation was determined according to the following criteria: there is some substance to the asylum claim, at least in their own view;[47] they are not a risk to public safety; they do not have a previous record of non-compliance; and they are 'amenable to supervision', which means that they have a verified private address where they could live and an individual or a community group willing to act as their 'community sponsor'.[48] Every participant in the AAP had a caseworker responsible for them and also a field officer who visited them to verify, both by appointment and through spot-checks, where they were living.

The AAP provided supervision at two levels. Intensive supervision participants were people initially detained by the INS immigration service and then released to the AAP. They had to report regularly to AAP supervision officers in person and by phone. Programme staff monitored each participant and re-evaluated the risk of absconding. Where appropriate, supervision measures were reduced after a period of compliance. Those included in the regular supervision scheme were originally sent written reminder notices about upcoming court obligations, although the AAP learned from the ongoing research on appearance rates that the basic notification model was less effective. The AAP decided that, in addition to written and oral reminders of court dates and other legal obligations, it would also provide information about the advantages of compliance and the consequences of non-compliance at each step of the process. For reminders to make a difference, those receiving them must already have a basic understanding of their obligations. To ensure that this was the case, those in both supervision programmes received information about immigration proceedings and the consequences of non-compliance, reminders of court hearings, and referrals to legal representatives and other services (Sullivan et al 2000).

The AAP ended in March 2000, by which time it had supervised more than 500 individuals who fell into three groups: people seeking asylum; individuals facing removal as a result of a criminal conviction, most of whom were lawful permanent residents (criminal aliens); and undocumented workers apprehended at work sites. In 1999, the INS had estimated that only 50 per cent of non-citizens released into the community appeared in court. Statistics also showed that those not detained pending their required departure from the country had a compliance rate of 11 per cent (Sullivan et al 2000). The AAP reported an appearance rate of 93 per cent for asylum-seekers released through the programme. The most important

finding of the AAP therefore is that most people want to comply, and that good supervision is better able to ensure this compliance than the fear of detention. When the project began, practitioners, including judges and lawyers, insisted that no participant would come to court if he or she knew that he or she could be detained if the case was lost. In practice this proved not to be the case. Where necessary, it was possible to maintain close supervision even in the complex neighbourhoods of New York (Stone 2000).

Based on its research, the Vera Institute concluded that it is not necessary to detain asylum-seekers in order for them to appear for court hearings. Neither do asylum-seekers appear to need intensive supervision in order to comply. The Institute also found that there were significant financial benefits to its approach, with supervision costing 55 per cent less than the cost of detention. The AAP demonstrates that having a legal representative and community and family ties are the most important factors in compliance, and that this is especially so for asylum-seekers.

The most important issue, however, is how to make the supervision as *effective* as possible. This necessarily involves a balance of monitoring and compliance efforts on the one hand, and providing support and incentives to comply with requirements on the other. As an incentive to attend their supervision meetings and comply with supervision requirements, the AAP offered participants access to information, help in finding low-cost legal representation, and referrals to health, educational and social services. As the programme accumulated experience, it became more adept at recognising warning signs that a participant might be contemplating absconding. Supervision staff became increasingly able to recommend that participants be re-detained while they still had accurate information about their whereabouts and before they actually absconded.

In order to assess whether incentivised compliance programmes similar to the AAP could be an alternative to the detention of children in the UK context, it is important to understand the factors behind the programme's success. The project's evaluation shows that information provided by the AAP contributed to participants' evolving awareness of laws, options, and consequences of non-compliance. In addition, the sense of belonging to a programme served to ease feelings of alienation and motivated them to comply. In effect, the AAP's support mirrored the benefits of community release. The AAP evaluation concluded that the more non-citizens feel they are a visible, legitimate part of their adopted country and have a sense of belonging the more they are willing and motivated to respond with co-operation and compliance. This feeling of legitimacy stems from feeling 'within the system' and documented, as opposed to invisible or underground. The provision of information and support to asylum-seekers can make the asylum process more credible and sustainable and can enable families to make more informed choices about their future, including returning to their countries of origin independently or voluntarily where this is appropriate. This approach is holistic and works precisely because it is in place from the beginning of the process and not simply at the end when relationships of trust have not been developed or have broken down.

Almost all of the stakeholders and individuals we interviewed as part of our research were aware of the AAP and viewed it positively. There was also some awareness of the programme within the Home Office, although less understanding of how the programme worked or its outcomes. The evidence available to us suggests that the combination of certain measures – freedom from detention; a graduated scale of supervision; individual needs and risk assessments; and support, primarily through provision of information – provides an ideal model for creating an alternative approach that reduces the use of detention and that such an approach should be piloted with families in the UK. Although it may be resource intensive, it has benefits for the asylum process as a whole and could result in significant benefits overall. Any programme of incentivised compliance would need to be fully integrated into the asylum determination process and would require properly funded legal advice and representation to be made available from the beginning of the process.

4.6 Voluntary return

As has been suggested throughout this report, one of the principle justifications for the use of detention, including the detention of children, has been to effect forced removal from the UK once all legal channels to obtain leave to remain have been exhausted. The issue of return is inextricably linked to the quality of decision-making. Good decision-making reduces the number of those required to leave who should not be expected to and instils greater confidence in the consistency and integrity of the decision-making process as a whole. This in turn means that a negative outcome is more likely to be sustainable.

Our alternative approach to the detention of children outlined above is dependent upon a different approach to the role of contact and information in the decision-making process and on a co-operative relationship between the applicant and the Home Office. This approach is based on evidence that a two-way flow of information which results in the family being aware of their rights and obligations and all the options available to them is more likely to result in compliance with immigration procedures without the need to resort to the detention of children.

Information about the opportunities for returning voluntarily to the country of origin should, in our view, be included as part of this information process. In the UK context, there are currently two forms of return that are dependent on the co-operation of those leaving. Self-check-in allows for Removal Directions to be set, and for a family or individual to make their own way independently to the airport. There is no evidence available on the extent to which self-check-in functions now, or on factors that may make self-check-in more likely. Voluntary assisted return involves the provision of support and assistance to enable return to be undertaken. The objective is to support the individual or family during the process of returning to their country of origin, and in some cases subsequently, in order that this return is durable.

Voluntary return is not strictly an alternative to detention, especially for those who do not agree that their case has been fully considered or for whom there are significant fears or anxieties about returning, despite the Home Office's decision that it is safe for them to do so.[49] When voluntary return is offered to detainees, such programmes may be described as 'alternatives to detention' but in reality constitute alternatives to trying to remain in the country (ECRE 1997). Although informing detainees of their rights and enabling voluntary return from within removal centres may be desirable and appropriate in some cases, any policy change in this regard must take into account the impact of detention on both those detained and other affected individuals. 'Voluntary' return may seem attractive when compared to remaining in detention for an indeterminate length of time (Ashford 1993; Noll 1998; Cole 2003). For the same reason, voluntary return is not strictly a safeguard for preventing the prolonged detention of children once a decision to detain has been taken.

Nonetheless if, as we suggest, the provision of information is crucial for enabling those who apply for asylum or other forms of leave to remain to better understand the processes in which they are involved, then it is important that information about mechanisms for returning to the country of origin in the event of a negative decision are included in this process. The Government recognises that voluntary return is the more sustainable and preferable approach to forced returns. It is also considered the best option by UNHCR, as one of its three durable solutions.

In February 1999, the Voluntary Assisted Return Programme (VARP) was established, funded by the Home Office and EU Refugee Fund. It is implemented by the International Organisation for Migration (IOM) in partnership with Refugee Action. The programme is open to asylum-seekers and failed asylum-seekers, or those with Exceptional Leave to Remain (ELR), Humanitarian Protection or Discretionary Leave. Since then VARP has developed a reintegration programme, and is now called VARRP (Baldaccini 2004). From September 2000 to August 2001, 1,033 asylum-seekers returned through VARP. The target was 1,200 and in 2002, 1,196 individuals returned through the programme. An independent evaluation of the returns programme commissioned by the Home Office found that it provided significant

cost savings for IND compared to forced removals (Home Office 2002).

We identified some concern both within and outside the Home Office that voluntary return options are currently under-utilised and undervalued. The fact that forced removal figures include dependants but those for voluntary return do not exacerbates this problem. Concerns about the process of referral to the programme, which were expressed in the Home Office's own evaluation, are further illustrated in HMIP case studies that reveal that some detainees in the UK wish to return but are unable to (HMIP 2002). Evidence produced during the House of Commons Home Affairs Committee (2003) inquiry on asylum removals also raised questions about the availability of the programme. The Committee recommended that the VARP programme be opened up to detainees in removal centres, and otherwise brought to the attention of detainees. It further recommended that the Immigration Service advise asylum-seekers of the option of voluntary return from the beginning of the process.

Given the evidence from our own research about the lack of knowledge and understanding regarding voluntary return options among both asylum-seekers and voluntary sector organisations working with them, it seems appropriate that there should be greater efforts to provide information to asylum-seekers from the beginning of the determination process about their options for voluntary return. We understand that this is recognised by some parts of IND but that while this information may be made available at the induction stage, it is not currently more widely or easily available.

However, while there is clearly scope for increasing the availability of voluntary return, the true 'voluntariness' of a decision to return cannot be separated from the wider context, including access to support. The Home Office's own evaluation of the VARP project found that one-quarter of voluntary returns were motivated by 'push' factors associated with conditions of stay in the UK. Since that time these 'push' factors have arguably increased significantly, not least through cuts to support for asylum-seekers whose applications have been refused. Furthermore, under Section 9 of the Asylum and Immigration (Treatment of Claimants, etc) Act (2004), families who have failed in their asylum claims and do not have travel documents will be sent a letter saying that they need to leave. The incentive to return 'voluntarily' will be the removal of support and the risk that children will be taken into care.

These concerns about the voluntariness or otherwise of options for return at the end of the asylum determination process reinforce the overall argument made in this section that information provision needs to be built into the alternatives that are made available to asylum-seekers from the very beginning of the application and throughout the determination process. The more that this information can be provided in partnership and through a wide range of different sources – including individualised caseworkers and legal representatives – the more likely will be the prospects of success in identifying and establishing genuine alternatives to the detention of children that focus less on control and more on facilitating and increasing contact and co-operation.

Key findings

- Despite the fact that the detention of asylum-seeking children contravenes international standards, and despite evidence about the negative impacts on children, immigration detention is treated as a low-risk strategy for securing compliance. This report identifies a range of alternatives to detention which maintain contact and compliance through mechanisms to provide support and information, and enhance the quality and credibility of the asylum determination process overall. Improved information flows can improve contact between asylum-seekers and the decision-making authorities so that the detention of children becomes unnecessary.

- The decision about whether or not it would be appropriate to separate a child from his or her parents or carers as an alternative to detention, needs to be carried out on a case-by-case basis to ensure that the decision made is in the best interests of the child.

- Alternatives to detention are meaningful only if they exist within a broader system of decision-making which ensures ongoing and consistent contact is maintained, and where asylum-seekers have information about their rights and are aware of their obligations. Quality legal advice and representation can provide an important mechanism for ensuring compliance by establishing confidence in the decision-making process generally and by making applicants aware of their rights and obligations, acting as a conduit for flows of information between the applicant and the Home Office and for ensuring that families are aware of all the choices and options available to them, including information on voluntary assisted return and reintegration programmes.

- There is currently a limited and inconsistent flow of information between the decision-maker and the applicant during the decision-making process. Although the use of reporting has increased in the UK over recent years, there are difficulties with the current approach because it is often not user-friendly, especially for families with children, and is approached principally as a mechanism for controlling the whereabouts of asylum-seekers rather than as a co-operative, two-way process for maintaining contact and as an alternative to detention. If things go wrong, for whatever reason, there is an assumption that the family or age-disputed individual has deliberately lost contact or failed to comply.

- The alternatives to detention discussed in this report focus on developing mechanisms for improving contact by providing support and information and on enhancing the quality and credibility of the asylum determination process overall. These mechanisms include reporting, electronic monitoring, supervised accommodation, community supervision and incentivised compliance.

- The mechanisms vary significantly in the extent to which contact between the applicant and the decision-maker is a two-way process that also provides support and information to the applicant. Approaches that provide most support and information are more likely to open up genuine alternatives to the detention of children and to have beneficial impacts on the asylum determination process more generally.

- Current approaches to reporting and electronic monitoring enable contact to be improved but deliver little if anything in terms of meaningful contact or the two-way provision of information. Supervised accommodation can meet this objective but can have similar negative impacts on children to those seen in detention. Community supervision has the potential to offer a meaningful alternative but only if available from the beginning of the decision-making process and not once a decision to detain has already been taken.

- The most effective alternative to the detention of children is the use of mechanisms for incentivised compliance similar to those seen in Sweden and piloted in the United States. These approaches provide a combination of freedom from detention, a graduated scale of supervision, individual needs and risk assessments and support, primarily through provision of information, legal advice and representation from the beginning of the asylum determination process.

- Options for voluntarily return are currently under-utilised and undervalued. While care must be taken to ensure that return under these circumstances is truly voluntary, there is considerable scope for improving the provision of information about the choices available to families at the end of the decision-making process. This has the potential to reduce further the perceived need to detain families in order to facilitate their removal from the UK.

Recommendations

- Case-by-case assessments should be carried out to establish whether it would be better for the child to be detained with his or her family, or separated. Parents and children should be part of this assessment in line with Article 12 of the UNCRC which gives children and young people rights to participate in decisions affecting their lives.

- Existing reporting mechanisms should be made more user-friendly and should be flexible to the needs of families with children. The Home Office should cover the financial costs of all reporting requirements. Where reporting arrangements break down, efforts should be made to re-establish contact before any decision is made to detain.

- The Home Office should pilot a system of incentivised compliance, based on a reporting system that incorporates support, information, legal advice and representation and meaningful contact. This system should be based on the Appearance Assistance Program (AAP).

- Information about the opportunities for returning voluntarily to the country of origin needs to be made more widely available throughout the decision-making process in order that families are aware of all the options that are available to them if a negative decision is finally reached. Return under these circumstances must be truly voluntary in order for it to be effective and durable.

Notes

44 See Ministerial Statement by Des Brown MP of 16th Sept 2004 on fast track asylum and detention policy available at www.parliament.the-stationery-office.co.uk/pa/cm200304/cmhansrd/cm040916/wmstext/40916m02.htm#40916m02.html_spmin0

45 To date more than 150,000 asylum-seekers have been issued with Asylum Registration Cards and a number of pilot projects are being carried out in different parts of the country using much more active contact management with people throughout the process (Baldaccini 2004)

46 IND statement on the Act Implementation Process (undated), available at

www.ind.homeoffice.gov.uk/ind/en/home/laws___policy/legislation/act_implementation.html

47 The assessment is based not on the objective strength of the asylum-seeker's claim, but rather whether the asylum-seeker *thinks* he or she has a good case, on the basis that as long as the asylum-seeker *believes* the claim to be a deserving one then he or she will go to appointments and is unlikely to abscond.

48 This person or group is not legally or financially responsible; it is a sponsorship involving time and effort rather than money.

49 A wide range of countries are considered by the Home Office to be safe for asylum-seekers whose applications have been refused to return to. These include Iraq, Somalia, the Democratic Republic of Congo and Zimbabwe.

5 Safeguards for detained children

In the previous sections of this report we presented an alternative approach for securing compliance with UK immigration controls that would remove the perceived need to detain children in the UK for the purpose of immigration control. This approach requires that children in families be excluded from fast track procedures, that improved contact and information flows are developed based on the tried and tested model of the AAP, and that there is a proper mechanism for formal age assessments to be undertaken by an independent panel prior to any decision to detain. This alternative approach would result in better outcomes for children because it would take into account their needs and vulnerabilities as *children*. It would also have the effect of making the asylum decision-making process itself more credible and sustainable and enable people to make more informed choices about their future – including returning to their countries of origin independently or voluntarily where appropriate. To be effective, such an approach would need to be in place from the beginning of the process. By the time IND has made a decision to detain, the relationship between the family and the Home Office has, for a range of reasons, broken down to the extent that alternatives become unworkable.

It remains unclear whether there is the political and policy appetite within government to develop the alternatives to the detention of children that we propose. In this context it is important that appropriate safeguards are developed to ensure that where children are detained, this does not become prolonged and that the welfare of children is placed at the centre of decisions about the family's future. UNHCR's (1999) guidelines on detention clearly state that children should not be detained. As a result, they do not require any specific procedural safeguards to be put in place for children. The guidelines do, however, require general safeguards to be available, including prompt and full communication of the reasons for detention, access to free legal assistance and the existence of a process by which the decision to detain is subjected to an automatic review before a judicial or administrative body independent of the detaining authorities. Moreover, this should be followed by regular periodic reviews of the necessity for the continuation of detention. While safeguards such as these cannot negate the impacts of detention on children, they are essential for ensuring that Home Office policy on the detention of children is reflected in practice.

5.1 Time limits on detention

There is currently no statutory limit on the length of time that anyone, including children, can be detained under immigration powers. This, in conjunction with the lack of statutory criteria for detention, means that the UK has one of the most open-ended and unsupervised detention systems in Europe (Baldaccini 2004). As with the numbers of child detainees, the Government has been keen to reassure interested parties that the majority of children are detained for a very short period of time (a matter of a few days) and that those cases where detention has been lengthy are very much the exception. For example Baroness Scotland stated on April 27th 2004 that:

> *Between 27 February and 25 March 2004, 95 families were taken into detention. Of 99 other families, 69 families were removed and 30 were released. There have been 134 children removed or released. The average time that those 134 children spent in detention was 9.8 days.*[50]

As already discussed in Section One of this report, the limitations of snapshot data mean that it is not possible to identify the lengths of time that children are detained, either individually or on average. It is therefore not possible to conclude categorically that children are detained for no more than a few days. Indeed, our evidence suggests that this is often not the case. Children who are detained with their families as part of fast track procedures are routinely detained for between seven and ten days. It is rare that fast track procedures are shorter than this. There is no data relating to the lengths of time that children whose age is disputed are detained. While it is not appropriate, given the size of our sample, to give an average duration for the time detained, within the cases we have looked at the length of detention varied considerably between seven days on the one hand to 268 days at the other extreme. This case was particularly concerning because it involved a 17-year-old boy whose age was disputed and who was held in a police cell for two days before being sent to Tinsley House and then Harmondsworth where he remained for more than 260 days. Half of all our case studies were detained for more than 28 days, and in some cases significantly in excess of this.

Given what we know about the significant increase in the negative impacts of detention on children the longer that detention lasts, it is important that there are statutory limits on the period for which children are detained. Ministers have argued that a statutory time limit would make immigration control unworkable. Some stakeholders also expressed concerns that the introduction of time limits could result in more rigorous enforcement of removals from detention. There is already some evidence that people being forcefully removed are treated inappropriately and that removals are taking place before all legal remedies have been exhausted (see, for example, Medical Foundation 2004). Despite these concerns, it seems to us that if policies and safeguards are working as they should and children are detained only as a measure of last resort, there is no reason for detention to continue beyond a maximum period of seven days. If, for whatever reason, removal cannot be effected during that time, the family should be released from detention and alternative mechanisms re-established for maintaining contact and ensuring compliance. If a statutory limit is not introduced then the welfare assessment discussed later in this section should be undertaken at this time (ie, after seven days).

Evidence from other countries suggests that statutory limits on the length of time for which children can be detained are both appropriate and workable. In Sweden, for example, children under 18 can only be detained for a maximum of three days. In extreme cases, this can be extended to six days, but for the entire year of 1999, no children were held in detention for more than four days (Mitchell 2001). To this extent a statutory limit on detention is the 'ultimate safeguard' because it ensures that regardless of the immigration-related circumstances of a particular case, a child cannot be detained for more than a limited period of time.

5.2 Review procedures

According to ILPA and BID (2003: 1), it is unusual for someone to be detained without the existence of a power to detain:

> *What is more common is the situation where a power existed to detain the person at the outset, but the detention has* become *unlawful because it has continued longer than is reasonable for the statutory purpose. This is most common in removal cases. An example of detention becoming unlawful is the Immigration Service detaining someone for the purposes of removal but then, because of problems in that person's country of origin, or because of administrative delays in obtaining travel documents, the detention continues for many months without the Immigration Service coming any closer to actually removing the person (emphasis in original)*

In order to reduce the possibility of this occurring and the detention becoming unlawful, the decision to detain must be reviewed on a regular basis. In reviewing detention, the Immigration Service must consider whether detention remains justified given any changing circumstances in the case. Reviews are particularly important if it is not clear why the original decision to detain was made. Reviews should comprise grounds for detention, timescale, proposal for progressing the case, prospects of removal, and compassionate circumstances. Because reviews can contain a wide range of information they are usually not disclosed. In this sense they are separate from communications with detainees about the progress of their case.

5.2.1 Reasons for detention

One of the fundamental principles of lawful detention is the need to provide reasons for detention to the detainee.[51] There is also a common law duty to give reasons for detention on the grounds that if these are not known then it is not possible to verify whether the detention is in accordance with the law (ILPA and BID 2003). The Government stated in its 1998 White Paper that the Immigration Service should give written reasons for detention in all cases at the time of detention and thereafter at monthly intervals, or at shorter intervals in cases involving families (Home Office 1998). A statutory requirement to give reasons to a detainee is contained in Rule 9 of the Detention Centre Rules, which came into force in April 2001.

In December 2003, following the inspections of Dungavel by HMIP and HMIE and criticisms about the lack of processes for ensuring that children in families are not detained for prolonged periods, the Home Office introduced additional procedures for reviewing these cases. The Management of Detained Cases Unit (MODCU) within IND have taken on responsibility for ensuring that the initial decision to detain a family is properly informed and family cases are supposed to be reviewed within MODCU at day seven by a Higher Executive Officer (HEO), day ten by a Senior Executive Officer (SEO), and at days 14, 21 and 28 at Assistant Director (AD) level. In addition, cases should be reviewed in between these periods to make sure that action on, for example, judicial review, is progressed. An additional process of ministerial authorisation was introduced for children who are detained for more than 28 days. As a result, the express authority of the Immigration Minister is required to detain any child for longer than 28 days, and every week thereafter, and a senior Home Office official has oversight of all children in immigration detention to ensure that there are no administrative delays that might extend their detention.[52]

The failure to provide families with proper reasons for their detention raises significant concerns about the

effectiveness of these procedures. Previous research suggests that detained families are not always given initial meaningful reasons for their detention (Cole 2003). Fewer than one in five of the case files studied by Bruegel and Natamba (2002) had a copy of the IS9164 form setting out the reasons for detention. Where the monthly updates on reasons for detention are given to detainees, the content of these is often vague, inconsistent or meaningless. For example, it may be limited to a statement that detention is justifiable because Removal Directions have been set (Weber and Gelsthorpe 2000; Cole 2003).

Very few of the families or children whom we interviewed had any recollection of being given initial reasons for detention, and there was rarely any evidence from the other information we analysed that such a form had been given to either the detainee or his or her legal representative.

An exception to this is the copy of a monthly update form that was provided by Marcia, whose experiences and those of her children, Sylvie and John, were described earlier in this report. Although the monthly update states the date on which Marcia was detained, it does not refer to the two children who were later taken out of school and joined her at Oakington. Indeed, anyone reading this form would not know that Marcia's children were detained with her. It summarises the dates of her asylum application, refusal, appeal, dismissal of appeal, and refusal of leave to appeal to the tribunal. It notes that Removal Directions were deferred about two weeks after the date of detention due to a judicial review application, on which a decision is still awaited. It concludes: 'in the meantime you will continue to be detained but may be assured that your situation will be reviewed on a regular basis'. There are no specific reasons given for the initial detention, nor for maintaining detention. The form does, however, include specific information which indicates that removal could not take place within a short space of time since an application for judicial review was outstanding. This raises the question of why the family was detained in the first place.

5.2.2 The review process

The failure for proper reasons for detention to be provided to families with children raises particular issues about the process by which reasons for the initial decision to detain are reviewed. This is critical for ensuring that detention does not become prolonged. There is some evidence, however, that reviews can be hampered by what Weber and Gelsthorpe (2000) describe as 'organisational inertia' and that cases can become 'institutionalised'. These concerns are shared by HMIP, whose inspections have indicated that immigration officers on site often do not know, and do not communicate, how cases are progressing. Neither is it evident that cases are being progressed efficiently (HMIP 2002). This view is supported by other research, which has found evidence that even when decisions are finally reviewed and reversed, there is often no apparent logic to the actions taken. People may, for example, be released without explanation some days after an unsuccessful bail hearing. Detainees often do not know why they have been released any more than they understand why they were detained. Many are under the impression that release decisions are arbitrary.

There were examples within our evidence base of cases where children in families appear to have been subject to unnecessary lengthy periods of detention because procedures for reviewing the decision to detain are ineffective. Joyce and Edwyn were detained for 116 days even though travel documents were not in place when the initial decision was taken to detain the family (see below).

In the case of Natlee and Enroy and their two daughters, detention became prolonged after it became clear that there were issues affecting the ability of the family to return to their country of origin that, for a variety of different reasons, had not previously been taken into consideration.

In these kinds of cases it appears that assumptions about the imminent prospect of resolving legal and practical issues preventing the family's removal, dominate the review process. Families find themselves in detention for another week, then another month. While there may be no explicit intention at the outset to detain the family for a lengthy period of time, in practice this can and does

Joyce and Edwyn (four months)

Joyce has been in the UK since late 2001. She initially arrived as a visitor but became an overstayer. She claimed asylum shortly after her son Edwyn was born and was told to return to the Home Office a few days later. When she did, she and her son, who was four months old at that time, were taken to Oakington. The family's application was dealt with under the NSA fast track procedures and refused. Joyce was served with Removal Directions 15 days after she was first detained and at the same time, she was informed that she would continue to be detained because she was likely to abscond if released and also because her removal was imminent. It was also stated she did not have enough close ties to the UK and that she had previously failed to comply with conditions of stay.

About one month after she was detained, Joyce says she was asked to produce Edwyn's birth certificate, but she was unable to do so. Two months later Joyce was informed that her detention would continue and that arrangements were being made to secure travel documents for her and her son. Nine days later her solicitors requested that she and Edwyn be released on Temporary Admission but this was refused on the basis that she was an overstayer with no close ties in the UK and no in-country right of appeal. Joyce and Edwyn remained at Oakington for a total of 116 days and were released two days before a second bail hearing was due. It appears that it was not possible to secure travel documents to return the family to their country of origin.

happen through an incremental process. Existing procedures for reviewing the decision to detain are not necessarily effective in preventing this from happening because they are conducted internally within IND and based primarily on immigration-related factors as opposed to information about the welfare of the child.

5.2.3 Ministerial authorisation

The process of ministerial authorisation adds little to the existing safeguards because it too is an internal review that appears to be based on the information that is already available to MODCU. There is no research evidence on the implementation of the ministerial authorisation process or the reviews on which they are supposed to be based. Neither is there any statistical information on how many such authorisations have been sought and how many granted or declined. There are no known cases where ministerial authority has been withheld in the case of a detained child. Much of the limited information that is available on the workings of the ministerial authorisation safeguard can be found in a July 2004 letter from Lord Bassam to Lord Avebury. Ministerial authorisations are not communicated to detainees or their representatives. This is because, according to Lord Bassam, "these are internal review processes and do not constitute formal decisions which need to be communicated to the family concerned, who will in any case receive monthly updates on their case and the reasons for detention".[53] This information also indicates that the minister is not automatically provided with the complete file of individual cases but instead provided with a comprehensive summary by MODCU.

The lack of transparency in the process by which ministers authorise the continuing detention of children beyond 28 days, has given rise to concerns among stakeholders that ministerial authorisations are based on immigration-related criteria alone. These concerns are exacerbated by the continuing absence of welfare assessments, despite a commitment that these would be taken into account in the authorisation process. With the exception of three families, all of the case studies in our sample were detained after the process of ministerial authorisation was introduced in December 2003. More than half of these families (14 out of 25 cases) were detained for longer than 28 days and it can only be assumed that their continuing detention was authorised by the minister in each case. Nine of these families were subsequently granted Temporary Admission. Several of these cases raised significant concerns about how the decision to continue detaining the family had been made, given the available evidence about the facts of the case. Perhaps no other case exemplifies these concerns more than that of Esma and Dermo, who were detained with their daughters Nina and Sibel (see page 59).

5.2.4 Review process for age-disputed children

Concerns about the detention of children whose age is disputed have been raised throughout this report. It is important to note that none of the existing safeguards extend to these children. Worse still, there is evidence to suggest that these children, who are exceptionally vulnerable, are being failed by routine review procedures applied to adult detainees. In some of our case studies – most notably that of Jacques which was described in detail earlier in this report – existing internal review mechanisms simply failed to prevent the prolonged detention of someone with severe mental health problems, despite the fact that these were clearly exacerbated by the detention process. Jacques told us:

> I got a review every week. Every time they said I should stay there for seven more days.

It was only when an advisor from the Refugee Council Children's Panel visited Jacques that any action was taken and he was moved to the hospital wing at Harmondsworth. There was still no independent assessment of his age and he was still not released for a further two and a half months. Even if Jacques were an adult, his treatment would have been unacceptable. The fact that Jacques was actually a separated child makes this case particularly shocking.

Esma, Dermo, Nina (aged seven) and Sibel (aged five)

Esma and Dermo arrived in the UK with their baby daughter Nina in 1998. They applied for asylum on arrival. The family's asylum application was refused about six months later. One year later, the couple had a second daughter, Sibel. At the end of 2001, the family made an application to remain in the UK on human rights grounds, but this was refused a day later. The family appealed, but this appeal was dismissed. The family was granted leave to appeal to the IAT. Before the Tribunal appeal had been heard, Esma was detained for ten hours at Gatwick, but was released. At the end of 2003, the Tribunal dismissed the family's appeal. Shortly afterwards Esma began regular counselling sessions.

About six months later the family was detained. Esma was pregnant at this time and Nina and Sibel were attending school. Although Dermo can speak English and the girls have largely grown up in the UK, Esma does not speak English. Esma attempted suicide while at Oakington, apparently on the family's first day there. The family was moved to Dungavel, and a first attempt was made to remove them but this was stopped due to Esma's poor health. Three days later another attempt to remove was made. Esma was experiencing pain and anxiety and the captain of the plane refused to carry her.

Two weeks after the family's detention, there was an application for judicial review. Esma's mental health continued to deteriorate and around a month after the family had been detained, Esma was sectioned under the Mental Health Act and taken to hospital. She was five months pregnant. Esma was particularly anxious about her unborn child and reported that she could not feel any movement. She was returned to Dungavel, where it was confirmed that she had miscarried. She was treated in the maternity ward of a hospital, and then sectioned again under the Mental Health Act.

While Esma was in hospital, Dermo and the couple's daughters were released on Temporary Admission and housed in a temporary hostel in Glasgow. They had been detained for about one month. Esma was released from hospital but returned to Dungavel. Two independent medical reports emphasised her suicidal risk and her increased chances of recovery if allowed to be with her husband and children. However, she was not released and, concerned about his daughters' education and their living conditions, Dermo and the children returned to London where they had been living before they were detained. Dermo reported at a reporting centre every day. He and the children were unable to visit their mother.

Over the following weeks Esma's solicitor and BID applied for her release on Temporary Admission on four separate occasions. Each was refused. An application for bail was then made and opposed by the Home Office on the grounds that Esma and her family had shown little incentive to return to their country of origin voluntarily. A second bail application made two weeks later was successful and Esme was released on Temporary Admission. She had been detained for 121 days.

5.2.5 Effectiveness of the review process

This evidence leads us to conclude that while procedures for reviewing the decision to detain already exist, these do not appear to respond automatically to changes in circumstances, including where obstacles to removal have arisen or been identified. One explanation for this is that those carrying out reviews at MODCU never see the detainees themselves. It is the staff in removal centres who see how the detainee is really doing, and they do not take part in the review. Although there are some provisions for communication between removal centre staff and IND, there is no requirement for IND to act on the information provided. Although the process of ministerial authorisation appears at first glance to be an important high-level mechanism for ensuring that the detention of children does not become prolonged, the absence of proper information about how the decision is made and the evidence on which it is based means that it is not possible to assess whether or not it is an effective safeguard against the negative impacts for children associated with prolonged detention. Safeguards are only effective if the information on which they are based is transparent and available for external scrutiny. To this extent, the ministerial authorisation process will always be limited as a review mechanism because it is not an independent review of the decision to detain as required by the UNCRC and UN standards on detention.

By contrast, in countries such as Canada, there are rights to automatic and then periodic review of detention (after 48 hours or without delay thereafter, then seven days, then every 30 days) by a member of the Immigration Division of the Immigration and Refugee Board (the quasi-judicial refugee status determination authority). Our evidence suggests that a similar independent process of review should be put in place in the UK, if the Government is serious about ensuring that the detention of children is a measure of last resort and takes place for the shortest possible length of time. Such a review would need to take into account all aspects of the decision to detain, related not solely to the possible or anticipated immigration-related outcomes but the welfare outcomes for the child arising from his or her continuing detention.

5.3 Legal safeguards

In the absence of a statutory time limit on the length of detention and any independent review process for the ongoing decision to detain, legal safeguards are a vital mechanism for ensuring that the detention of children is a last resort and for the shortest possible time. The report of the Joint Committee on Human

Rights into the 2002 Nationality, Immigration and Asylum Bill concluded that "safeguards are meaningful and effective only if appropriate legal advice and information are available to detainees" (Joint Committee on Human Rights 2002: para. 87). While some legal safeguards exist, our research raises serious concerns about how to make them meaningful and accessible in a context where access to quality legal advice and representation on immigration issues has become a rare commodity. This general problem – which is due largely to the increasingly strict limits that have been placed on the financial rewards available to those who provide a quality service in this area – is exacerbated for those in detention at precisely the time when such advice is most needed.

5.3.1 Access to legal advice and representation

HMIP has expressed concerns that detainees are not easily able to obtain competent independent legal advice to explain their situation or represent them (HMIP 2002). According to information collated by AVID, in December 2003, 13 per cent of their clients did not have legal representatives, and children were the least likely to have representatives. BID also has broad concerns about the accessibility of legal advice and representation for detainees, in particular for the 12 per cent detained solely under immigration powers in criminal prisons and for detained families.

It is clear that the cost of representing a detainee is significant. Consultation with detained asylum-seekers is much more burdensome than with non-detained clients. The investment of time and resources is multiplied when the lawyer needs the assistance of either an interpreter or a medical expert. In addition, asylum-seekers are sometimes transferred from one detention centre to another. The transfers are often accomplished without any prior notice to the detainee, their friends or relatives, or even their legal representatives. Solicitors may feel unable to visit due to time-constraints imposed by their workload, and the difficulty and costs of travelling to detention centres. If there are Removal Directions in place, solicitors may consider a visit even less worthwhile (Pistone 1999; Cole 2003).

Our findings indicate that there are very significant difficulties experienced by many detainees in accessing quality legal advice and representation. This raises important issues about the ability of families with children and individuals whose age is disputed to gain access to any of the existing safeguards that are in place to ensure that detention is lawful and does not become prolonged. This problem was particularly evident in relation to the Dungavel Removal Centre where factors such as those described above have led the Immigration Advisory Service (IAS) based in Glasgow to reduce significantly the amount of work undertaken for detainees being held in the centre. Dungavel is located some 25 miles outside Glasgow and can only be accessed by car. This entails significant additional travelling time and associated costs. The need to travel to the isolated centre, go through security procedures, and sometimes have an enforced break as no one other than staff or detainees may be on-site during mealtimes, after which security procedures must be undergone again, also contributed to the difficulties of providing representation to detainees. Moreover, although the Scottish Legal Aid Board is independent of the Westminster Legal Services Commission and is not as limited in what it will fund, there are difficulties related to the fact that most detainees in Scotland will have been taken there from England, and will need either to communicate with their original legal representatives at great distance, or find new representatives under a different system.

5.3.2 Quality of legal advice

Only at Oakington is there on-site and properly regulated specialist legal advice and representation.[54] However, even being detained at Oakington does not guarantee that a family will be properly represented.

Barbara and Sammy (aged ten months)

Barbara came to the UK in 2000 having left her country of origin following threats from violent gangs. She left her son behind with family members. In 2001 Barbara met John, a British citizen and at the end of 2002 they had a son, Sammy. Barbara claimed asylum at the end of 2003. She and Sammy were taken to Oakington where the case was dealt with under NSA procedures and refused.

Although she had never previously seen a legal representative about her case, Barbara had five separate sets of legal representatives while in detention. The first solicitor demanded £1,000 in fees to apply for bail. Not only did Barbara not have access to such funds, she was suspicious of the request and changed representatives. Although she only spoke to the second solicitor on the phone, he obtained Barbara's papers and contacted her sister in the UK, to request money. When Barbara's sister refused, the solicitor visited Barbara and demanded £350 to return her papers to her. Following this experience, Barbara instructed a third solicitor, who came to visit her and said she would help, but never got back in touch. When Barbara enquired, the solicitor's office said her case was finished. The fourth solicitor also demanded money. Barbara says that none of the legal representatives asked her about her reasons for claiming asylum, and did not provide her with any information or advice about the process and her options.

Barbara was still at Oakington when she instructed the Refugee Legal Centre to represent her. Removal Directions were cancelled after Barbara made an application for Judicial Review. She and her son were then transferred to Dungavel. She received little notice of the transfer, and had to prepare a statement over the telephone after her arrival there. Although she received assistance from BID to prepare for a bail hearing, Barbara and her son were released on Temporary Admission later that month. They had been detained for 161 days.

The case of Barbara and Sammy is illustrative of this (see page 61). From the evidence we have seen, it appears that Removal Directions were not served on Barbara until she and her son had been in detention for nearly five months and that the legal representatives who were instructed to represent the interests of her and her son failed to do so.

Unfortunately, this family's experience of poor quality or unscrupulous legal representation was not unique among our case studies. Indeed, evidence of this problem was considerable and was not limited to the time spent in detention but also occurred prior to detention – in some cases contributing to it – and subsequently. Examples include:

- advising a client not to include certain information in a statement, leading to an incomplete account
- not asking why the applicant left their country of origin
- leaving clients to represent themselves at appeals without any notice
- getting paperwork signed, presumably in order to obtain legal aid payment, and then doing nothing
- giving incorrect or misleading information
- failing to make an application for bail
- demanding substantial cash payments to make bail applications
- obtaining papers from a previous representative without consent.

5.3.3 Legal advice for age-disputed children

These impacts of incompetent or unscrupulous legal advice and representation appear to be particularly significant for children whose age is disputed, not least because it can mean that the decision to detain is not challenged and no independent age assessment sought. Daren told us that he had had difficulties in finding a legal representative because as soon as he arrived in the UK he was detained at Dungavel, where there is no on-site legal advice and representation. Once he had been able to access a solicitor, there appears to have been poor communication about the progress of the case. Daren was not given a copy of his statement in advance of the appeal hearing and was not in a fit state to read it at that time. It turned out to contain errors.

[In Tinsley House] we contacted a new solicitor. The assistant came. It wasn't the person we called. We were not sure. She said, 'What are your problems?' I told her everything, but not the problem about my age. She said she would come and see us. She said she would get bail, for release. I don't know . . . nothing happened. She came back two or three weeks later for me to sign papers, to pay them. I was thinking, she hasn't done anything yet, but I signed . . .[Following a transfer to Harmondsworth] I called the solicitor to say I was in a new place. Another man came, who also got me to sign for payment. [. . .] The solicitor said I had to go to court. The solicitor didn't come to court. There were people there – one man at a table. They showed me this paper and asked if everything was true. My body was shaking, I didn't know what to say, I didn't get to read the paper. They gave it to me to read, but I couldn't. I only read it two or three days later and when I read it, it was wrong . . . After three days I got a letter saying they didn't believe me, also about my age, and they were taking me back.

There was evidence in one case of a legal representative telling his client not to raise the issue of his age being incorrect. Bem was 16 when he was detained at Dungavel. The people who smuggled him into the UK told him to say that he was 18 years old. When he was transferred to Harmondsworth, Bem told an immigration officer that he was a child but the date of birth was not changed on his forms. His legal representative failed to deal appropriately with the issue of his disputed age and the fact that he could be a child:

[In Harmondsworth] they said they would find a lawyer for my case. I said I didn't know how to find a lawyer. My solicitor came. I told him what happened about my age. He said I should forget about that, that if I tried to change my date of birth to my real one it would complicate my case.

Following this meeting, Bem was befriended by a fellow national who was concerned for his welfare. Bem explained what had happened with the legal representative. When challenged about his actions, the legal representative refused to represent him anymore.

I was crying. This man came up to me because I was sitting down and crying. He asked me where I was from, and he too was [the same nationality]. He asked about my solicitor. I had his card. The Nigerian took his money and called the solicitor. He asked the solicitor why he had made me stick to my date of birth. The solicitor put down the phone. He didn't answer the question. After a few days he came with a letter saying he couldn't continue my case. I would find another solicitor. I was just confused, I didn't know what to do. The man said the solicitor was a wicked man, and that I should not have been in there. I was crying. He said I should not cry. He gave me the telephone number for BID and said I should tell them what happened. I called BID, and told them what happened and what the solicitor said.

BID alerted the Refugee Council Children's Panel to the fact that Bem was being detained in Harmondsworth. The Panel arranged for an age assessment interview to be undertaken. Bem was found to be a child and released into the care of social services the same day. He had been in detention for 48 days.

They interviewed me. It was two people, with an interpreter because I didn't hear much English. They asked me questions – my mother and father's name. I told them my father died when I was going to school, my mother died when I was ten. At the end they asked me my date of birth. They said I am a young person and they would take care of me. I said, 'when?' They said they would make a telephone call. They said they would take me out that night. It was seven or eight. They asked me to get my bag and clothes. But I didn't have anything, just what I was wearing, and a towel and a jumper from the detention centre. They left, and sent a taxi for me. The Immigration people gave me a small paper. I was happy.

Because there is no systematic provision of legal advice and representation across the detention estate and there is no process for systematically assessing those whose age is disputed, children like Bem only end up coming to light because other detainees are willing to help them and because organisations like BID exist and can refer cases to the Refugee Council Children's

Panel if this has not already been done, as it should, by IND. This raises questions about whether any of the existing or proposed mechanisms for safeguarding the interests of children in detention can be made to work without the introduction of a formal process for age assessment – as was proposed in Section Three of this report – and without improvements in the system for providing legal advice and representation. At a very minimum, financial thresholds should be reviewed to incorporate automatic additional time for representing detained clients. In Section Four we proposed a model of contact and information as the framework for providing alternatives to the detention of children. Within this framework, quality legal representatives can provide an important mechanism for ensuring compliance by: establishing confidence in the decision-making process generally; making applicants aware of their rights and obligations; acting as a conduit for flows of information between the applicant and the Home Office; ensuring that families are aware of all the choices and options available to them, including information on voluntary assisted return and reintegration programmes.

5.3.4 Bail

Detention can be challenged through bail application, application for habeas corpus or judicial review. Habeas corpus and judicial reviews are possible where, respectively, it is alleged that the detention is unlawful or the underlying administrative decision such as refusal of leave to enter is challenged (ILPA and BID 2003). Applications for bail can be made to the Immigration Appellate Authority, the local Chief Immigration Officer (CIO), or the Home Office. Although the Immigration and Asylum Act (1999) introduced automatic bail reviews for immigration detainees after eight days and 36 days, these were never implemented and were subsequently repealed in 2002. In the absence of automatic bail hearings, the onus is on detainees to know about the process of seeking bail, and to secure legal representation in order to access it.

Bail is an important legal safeguard for ensuring that children are not detained for prolonged periods. Our evidence suggests that this is not only because of the hearing itself, but because an application for bail effectively triggers a review of the detention decision. An application for bail requires IND to produce a bail summary setting out its reasons for opposing bail. In this sense it 'concentrates the mind' and may trigger release from detention even before the bail application is heard. This is reflected in the fact that a number of families were released before a bail hearing, even though continuing detention had been authorised by the minister not long before. Four families in our case studies had been released on Temporary Admission shortly after bail preparations had begun. Detention periods for these four cases ranged from 32 to 161 days, with an average time of 87 days. In one case, a bail hearing had already taken place and bail granted in principle, pending production of evidence from the surety at a future listed hearing. In the case of Annette, Lauren and Khamisi which was outlined earlier in this report, the family was released one day after a visit from an independent doctor, having being detained for 41 days.

However, even where a case is reviewed before a bail hearing this does not necessarily lead to the end of detention, even where the available evidence suggests that it should. Jacques suffered from severe mental health problems before and during his detention at Harmondsworth for nearly nine months. Regular reviews undertaken every seven days failed to result in his release. Three months after he was detained, Jacques' solicitor told him that bail would not be possible. It was not until the visit from the Children's Panel adviser that the first bail application was made. The Home Office opposed this application:

My solicitor didn't help me. It is the same solicitor I have now. He never came to visit me. He said there was not enough money on my file . . . [After the visit from the Children's Panel adviser] my solicitor asked for a medical report from the centre, to ask for bail. It took one month for this to happen . . . The Refugee Council acted as a surety for me. I think I looked bad when I came to the court for bail. I was wearing a sheet. The judge was angry with the Home Office and asked how they could detain someone who was sick. I was given bail.

Reasons given by the Home Office for opposing bail also appear contradictory in some cases, as in the example below.

5.3.5 The bail application process

As the evidence already presented in this report suggests, families and children whose age is disputed are ill-informed about judicial processes, including bail. In BID's experience, the requirement for sureties and the application of the merits test for Controlled Legal Representation may in effect block access to bail. This is partly because some legal representatives believe that adjudicators require two sureties offering substantial amounts of money to secure bail, even though this is not a legal requirement and it is possible to obtain bail without them (ILPA and BID 2003). BID and other legal representatives with whom we spoke have obtained release on bail for many detainees who have no sureties or very low sureties. In other cases, legal representatives have refused to lodge a bail application for families detained with children on the basis that the application does not have a reasonable chance of success so would not pass the merits test for public funding. Shontelle, who was detained with her daughter, Leah, aged eight, told us that:

My solicitor said I needed £3,500 to apply for bail, and because I didn't have it, he didn't apply.

This evidence suggests that some legal representatives confuse the merits test for bail applications with the test that must be applied in order to access funds to represent the applicant in relation in the asylum claim. In fact, the prospect of success for each should be considered separately.

Recognising that legal safeguards are not meaningful in the absence of good quality legal advice and representation, some governments in other countries have attempted to establish more systematic processes for accessing bail. In Canada for example, the Government funds the Toronto Bail Program, an initiative specifically aimed at enabling immigration detainees to apply for bail. The programme is an adaptation of a scheme originally designed for people in the criminal justice system who could not afford bail and describes its aim as being to remove the element of financial discrimination from the bail

Cecilia, Samuel, Antonio (aged 18 months) and Amie (aged six weeks)

Cecilia and Samuel are from an African country. They arrived in the UK in 2002 and applied for asylum on arrival at the airport. Initially they made separate asylum claims, but later Cecilia withdrew her claim and was a dependant on her husband's claim. Samuel's asylum claim was refused two months after their arrival. Just under a year after their arrival, his appeal was also dismissed and leave to appeal to the Tribunal was refused. Samuel was required to report once a week throughout this time.

The couple had their first child, Antonio, in 2003 and as a result of a pastoral visit to the family, the Home Office learnt that Cecilia was pregnant again. Removal Directions were set for a date after the birth of the couple's second child. Six weeks after Amie was born, and seven months after the pastoral visit, the family was detained from their home. The family did not receive a second pastoral visit.

The bail summary records that Cecilia was 'distressed and uncooperative' on the day that the family was detained. Other records show that Cecilia was suffering from serious postpartum problems. She was bleeding, in significant pain, and had been due to have an operation ten days after they were detained. Her doctor had told Cecilia that the operation was urgent. While in detention Cecilia was given tablets to treat her condition, which she reported did not help.

A removal attempt was made four days after the family was detained. The bail summary states it was 'thwarted due to disruptive behaviour'. There is no mention of Cecilia's medical problems. A week later, on the advice of a legal representative at Oakington, Cecilia made her own asylum claim. The bail summary refers to this as 'another stalling tactic used by her to frustrate removal or at least to assist in the bail process.' BID applied for bail and received a bail summary. The bail summary stated that 'if the family were granted bail and issued with self-check-in Removal Directions, it would be extremely difficult for them to make their way to London with two infants and their belongings in order to catch their flight'. At the same it also stated that if the family were released from detention it was highly likely that they would abscond. It has never been alleged that they failed to report, or in any other way lost contact with the authorities. Following the failed removal attempt, a new removal date was set, with six escorts planned, about three weeks later. The family was removed from the UK on that date.

system (ECRE 1997). Programme supervisors consider applications from those who are deemed to pass all other tests such as security and identity, but who have no community ties from whom to raise the requisite bail money.

In the UK, by contrast, there is a disproportionate reliance on ad hoc support or voluntary organisations to provide access to those legal safeguards that currently exist. BID, for example, works with asylum-seekers and migrants detained under UK Immigration Act powers in removal centres and prisons. BID prepares and presents applications for bail and provides advice and information to detainees about how they can challenge their detention and obtain release. BID has produced a *Notebook for Bail* which provides information to detainees about their rights to challenge their detention, how to ask their representative to apply for bail for them, and provides details of how to represent themselves at bail applications if they are unable to find a legal representative to act on their behalf.

Since BID was set up in 1998, it has made over 1,000 bail applications and succeeded in securing release for over 600 people. BID is also aware of at least 30 people who have successfully represented themselves since December 2003. But this approach is far from ideal. BID is a charity reliant on volunteers with no public funding and clearly does not have the capacity to deal with all the cases about which it becomes aware. Moreover, BID is not embedded into the detention process as a formal mechanism for providing advice. There are likely to be many cases that BID never gets to hear about and who may not be known to anyone outside the Home Office. BID is also clear that only some detainees will be able to use the information they provide in lieu of a representative. This information is currently only available in English and French due to a lack of funding for translation. The use of the notebook for self-representation can be impeded by many factors. One of the mothers among our case studies, a fluent English-speaker, said she was too depressed and distracted to be able to use the information in the notebook although she was aware of it. For separated children whose age is disputed, the problems with self-representation are clear.

5.3.6 The failure of legal safeguards

The evidence presented in this section suggests that while legal safeguards such as bail exist, they are not easily accessed and are therefore are not a wholly effective mechanism for safeguarding the interests of children who are detained. These problems could be negated by the introduction of an automatic regular and independent review of the decision to detain. This review should follow a similar model to that utilised in Canada and set out in 5.2.5 above. In the absence of a regular independent review, access to legal representation for the purpose of preparing a bail application should be provided through a scheme similar to the Toronto Bail Program (see 5.3.5). Alternatively, a panel for the welfare of children could be established within each removal centre where families with children are held. This panel would be responsible for reviewing the welfare of children in detention and could ensure that a child is released from detention without the requirements associated with the bail application process where there was evidence that the child's welfare and well-being were being negatively affected.

5.4 Assessment of children's welfare and well-being

As has been noted throughout this report, HMIP is of the view that children who are subject to immigration control should not be detained, and that where they are, this should be for a maximum of a few days. In its report on Dungavel (HMIP 2002), HMIP recommended that there should be an independent assessment of the welfare, developmental and educational needs of each detained child and that this assessment should be used to inform decisions on detention and its continuation. In December 2003 the Government accepted this recommendation and proposed that welfare assessments would be introduced initially at Dungavel, where they would take place 21 days after a child was detained, and then rolled out to reception and removal centres in England, where detained children would have welfare assessments after 28 days detention.

Despite this commitment, a system for welfare assessments is not yet in place. Although IND has been in discussion with South Lanarkshire Council Social Services regarding the establishment of such a process at Dungavel, agreement has not yet been reached as to how this might operate in practice. According to IND staff whom we interviewed, this is because there are complex issues involved and it is important to get the system right rather than put something in place that could be inappropriate or unworkable. There are no procedures in place for making this happen in practice in Dungavel, Oakington or Tinsley House. In the meantime the detention of children is set to begin at Yarls Wood Removal Centre. It is understood that similar discussions with Bedfordshire Social Services have not yet begun. For children whose age is disputed by the Home Office these assessments would in any case not apply. The result is that reviews of the decision to detain, including the process of ministerial authorisation, continue to be based primarily on immigration-related criteria as opposed to evidence about the welfare and well-being of the child.

The Home Office has insisted that welfare issues are not overlooked in the review process and that removal centres holding families have properly trained staff and healthcare teams that are alert to any welfare issues that may arise for the children in their care. This is questioned in the report of HMIP's most recent visit to Oakington, published in November 2004, which found that although the centre made conscientious attempts to identify and support children at risk of harm, residential staff lacked the necessary qualifications, or support from social services. In addition, the report notes that agreed procedures for the detention of children were not being followed and there was no independent social service assessment of children staying longer than a few days, though files showed that some children were suffering distress. HMIP has reiterated its view that the welfare of children held for periods of over seven days should be independently monitored, in conjunction with social services (HMIP 2004).

5.4.1 The need for independent welfare panels

In light of the concerns expressed by HMIP and the evidence presented in Section Two of this report, we have proposed that a statutory time limit of no more than seven days be introduced for children who are detained with their families. In the current absence of a statutory time limit on the immigration detention of children, and in view of the evidence presented throughout this section about the effectiveness of existing review mechanisms or legal safeguards, we recommend that an independent welfare panel should be established. This should have responsibility for reviewing all decisions to detain children and for undertaking regular reviews of this decision. The welfare panel should assess the welfare of any child in detention at seven days then again at 21 days and at a regular period thereafter should detention become prolonged. This could be the same panel recommended in Section Three of this report to take responsibility for assessing the age of those individuals whose age is disputed. Given our recommendation for an alternative model to the detention of children based on contact and information, assisted appearance and community

supervision, this panel should have the power to release families and children whose age has been disputed from detention without the need to apply for bail.

In reviewing the decision to detain and to continue detention, the panel should take into account all aspects of a child's welfare and well-being together with information about the immigration-related issues in the case and the prospects of any outstanding issues being resolved quickly. Such a panel could draw on the evidence of a welfare officer based at the removal centre. Both HMIP and the House of Commons Home Affairs Committee (2003) have recommended that a welfare officer be attached to each removal centre with a remit that includes ensuring that those detained have an opportunity to alert friends, family and legal representatives to their impending removal. Although the Government did not accept this recommendation, it left open the possibility of reconsidering this issue in the light of any new evidence that existing procedures could be improved.

Given the evidence presented in this report about the issues associated with children whose age is disputed, it is also important that there are proper procedures in place if an individual is assessed as being under 18 years of age while in detention. There is evidence – both anecdotal and from our case studies – that being assessed as a child does not currently automatically mean that separated children are given appropriate care and assistance. Some children remain in detention pending a decision about where they will go. There is some anecdotal evidence that removal centre staff, not wanting to detain a child unlawfully, may simply send a child by public transport to the area where they were previously living or the port at which they entered the country. Local social services in that area may or may not be informed of their imminent arrival. These children can end up disappearing altogether or find themselves caught in a battle between different social service departments that refuse to take responsibility for them. The experiences of George are illustrative of this problem (see page 68).

5.4.2 Children first and foremost

It is important to reiterate that no amount of safeguards can guarantee that the welfare and well-

George (aged 16 years)

George arrived in the UK early in 2004. He was 16 years old and had been imprisoned and tortured in his home country. On his arrival, George was fingerprinted and held at the airport from mid-morning to evening. He was then released and told to report to the airport the following morning, which he did after sleeping rough. At his interview an immigration officer told him that his passport was false and that they would return him to his country of origin. They asked that he come back the following day. Afraid of being returned, George did not go back to the airport. Instead he spent money on hotels, and then slept rough for about two months. He met someone who was going to Leeds and joined them, but was not able to cope with the situation in which he found himself and went to the police. The police gave George directions and some money to get to the Refugee Council in Leeds who arranged for him to go to Heathrow to be interviewed by IND.

When he arrived for his interview, the issue of the false passport which George had used to enter the country was raised. His age was disputed and he was sent to Oakington where he remained for nearly a month. During this time his legal representative requested that Cambridgeshire Social Services make an age assessment. This was carried out 23 days after George arrived at Oakington. George was not informed of the outcome of the assessment, but he was released four days later. He was given directions to the Refugee Council in another town, and then put into emergency accommodation in Suffolk, arranged by the Refugee Council. Suffolk Social Services said that they would care for George if no one else would and George gave his permission for them to obtain a copy of the age assessment carried out by Cambridgeshire Social Services. This resulted in Suffolk Social Services claiming that Cambridgeshire Social Services were responsible for him. This issue has not yet been resolved.

being of children will be taken into account where the decision-making process is driven primarily by immigration criteria. Unlike other areas of law and practice, their experiences and status as children are not integral to the policies and processes by which they are treated. This marginalisation of their needs as children has resulted in a situation where the decision to detain has come to be based primarily on immigration control priorities and that once in detention, there is no duty of care to ensure that their needs are met.

There are, however, benchmarks for children's welfare that should apply equally to all children, including those subject to immigration detention. In October 2002, the Joint Chief Inspectors' report, *Safeguarding Children*, recommended that the Home Office issue revised guidance to Area Child Protection Committees (ACPCs) on the requirements and arrangements to safeguard children in prisons and Young Offender

Institutions, and emphasised that additional resources would be required (DoH 2002). Their report followed the commitment in the 1998 White Paper on *Modernising Social Services* that a review would be carried out every three years by all the relevant Chief Inspectors to ascertain how well children are being safeguarded. One month after the publication of *Safeguarding Children*, a landmark decision in the High Court held that the Children Act (1989) applies to children held in prison custody. The action was brought by the Howard League for Penal Reform to challenge the Home Office policy that the Children Act did 'not apply to under-18s in prison establishments'.[55] The decision means that local authorities retain a statutory duty to safeguard the welfare of children even if they are in prison.

One mechanism for reconnecting children subject to immigration control to other policies for protecting children in the UK is to include them within the remit of the Children's Commissioners for Northern Ireland, Wales, Scotland and, most recently, England. To date there has been government resistance to this approach on the basis that detention is a devolved or reserved matter over which the Children's Commissioners in Scotland, Wales and Northern Ireland have no jurisdiction. On being advised that the immigration detention of children at Dungavel falls outside her remit for protecting the interests of children and young people in Scotland, the Commissioner for Children and Young People in Scotland, Kathleen Marshall, commented to us that "children are not wholly defined by their immigration status; they are human beings with a whole spectrum of human rights. It is 'matters' that are reserved to Westminster, not children". It remains to be seen whether the new Commissioner for Children and Young People in England will have a role in relation to these children.

5.5 Protecting children from abuse

The detention of children raises a number of important child protection issues. Detained children are potentially at risk of abuse from other detainees, removal centre staff, or their own family members, in some cases because the overall impacts of detention on the mental health of families exacerbate the likelihood that parents will abuse their children. In addition, all of the case studies involving separated children whose age is disputed by the Home Office raise significant child protection concerns. These individuals are detained with adults and the staff with responsibility for them are not subject to enhanced checks.

As a result of concerns about the possible abuse of children who are detained, a child protection policy for the detention estate has been devised by the NSPCC, under contract to the IND. The NSPCC provides training and advice on child protection issues that might arise within the context of families who are detained. As part of this process the NSPCC has developed national standards in child protection for any child detained under immigration powers which are now in use in removal centres. This is a welcome development, as are reports that social services and the police are now involved where child protection concerns are raised.

5.5.1 Gaps in policy and practice

Despite these efforts, our research has found evidence of serious gaps in current policy and practice. In some cases, existing policies and procedures do not appear to be working as they should. In one of our case studies, for example, a family was detained and then removed despite the parents having an outstanding charge under Section 12 of the Children and Young Persons (Scotland) Act 1937, which refers to abuse or neglect of a child. Acts under this section are grounds for criminal proceedings and for compulsory measures of supervision under the Children (Scotland) Act 1995. The charge made against the parents was certainly known to IND at some stage because it was referred to in the family's bail summary. The bail summary also notes that ministerial authorisation for maintaining detention was granted after 28 days and every week after that. The family was removed from the UK without the outstanding child protection issues being resolved.

Our concerns about the effectiveness of existing policies are echoed in the HMIP's most recent report on its visit to Oakington (HMIP 2004). In this report, the Chief Inspector of Prisons, Anne Owers, raises concerns that although a detailed child protection policy has recently been published, the child protection committee had not met for almost a year and the families and children committee appeared not to have met since 2002. Moreover, although all staff are trained in child protection, not all staff working in the family unit had undergone enhanced Criminal Records Bureau (CRB) checks. According to the NSPCC this issue is now being addressed. In some cases, HMIP found no evidence that immigration officers who were responsible for determining who was admitted to the centre, carried out any checks to establish whether a child was at risk or on a child protection register. Nor was any screening carried out on adults who were being admitted to the establishment. Moreover, where child protection issues were raised, referral to the local social services department was slow and in need of improvement.

In addition to general concerns about the effectiveness of child protection policies, there is also some evidence that measures to address potential child abuse risks may actually exacerbate the risks of abuse because they do not acknowledge the impacts of detention on parents' levels of stress and ability to look after their children. The Medical Foundation reports on one such example, where a woman was detained with her baby and her increasing depression led to her child's distress. She was put on 'watch', involving her door being banged on every three hours throughout the day and night, which contributed to greater distress for the mother.

The principle of the child protection policies devised by the NSPCC for the detention estate has been one of extending existing provisions to children in detention. These policies do not reflect or respond to the possibility of damage being caused by detention itself and have been criticised by the Medical Foundation and others for failing to take into account the very important differences between the environment in which children are detained and other contexts.

A child protection audit undertaken by the NSPCC in October 2004 also highlighted many of the deficiencies we have identified. Since that time we understand that the Detention Policy Unit have agreed to seek changes and are raising issues with the contractors. These changes should take into account the findings of our research.

5.5.2 Protection of separated children

It is our understanding that the NSPCC's remit does not extend to child protection issues that might arise in cases involving separated children whose age is disputed. This is a crucial gap in current efforts to protect children from abuse. Research undertaken by Ayote and Williamson (2001) notes that these children express concern about being detained with other adults. These concerns were shared by some of the children in our case studies. Bem's comments highlight the vulnerabilities that these children face

and the additional risks to which they are currently subjected whilst in detention. Bem was 16 when he was detained with adults at Harmondsworth:

I have never been in detention before coming to the UK. I had problems before here . . . I was raped and abused. In detention, I was with these men, adults, in my room. I wanted to watch cartoons but they wouldn't let me. They wanted to watch news. If I wanted to play on the computer they would make me get off because they said I was not doing anything, I was just playing games . . . I didn't know anybody. The people were older than me and I was afraid to talk.

Daren was aged 16 when he was detained at Dungavel and subsequently transferred to Tinsley House and then Harmondsworth. He expressed similar concerns:

I was really afraid. Everyone there [in detention] was bigger and stronger than me. I walked slowly, didn't talk to them. I was scared. The way they talk, loud, to the officers. I just stayed on my own. [. . .] I felt bad. I almost killed myself but in the room there is nothing to use. And the police was always coming to see if someone is dead. I was just weak.

Evidence from our research suggests that the failure to undertake age assessments before detaining individuals whose age is disputed may put those who are subsequently found to be children at risk. In the absence of a policy not to detain age-disputed individuals unless and until an independent age assessment has been undertaken, any policies designed to address child protection issues in detention should take into account the very significant possibility that these individuals may in fact be children and therefore vulnerable to abuse from staff and other adults with whom they are detained. *All* staff – and not just those coming into contact with children in families – should undergo enhanced CRB checks. Children within families about whom there are age protection concerns should not be removed from the UK unless and until these issues are resolved.

Key findings

- Current UK policy and practice mean that children can and do remain in detention for lengthy periods. In the cases that were studied, the length of detention varied considerably from seven days to 268 days. Half of all cases looked at (16 in total) were detained for more than 28 days.

- The report raises significant concerns about the effectiveness of existing review procedures for ensuring that the detention of children is not prolonged. Existing safeguards do not appear to respond automatically to changes in circumstances, including where obstacles to removal have arisen or been identified.

- There is evidence that the review process is dominated by immigration-related issues and that the welfare of children is not a key consideration in the continuing decision to detain. This problem is exacerbated by the failure to introduce welfare assessments and by the absence of any external mechanisms for routinely reviewing decisions. The recently introduced process of ministerial authorisation adds little to the existing safeguards because it is an internal review that is based on information that is already available to the Home Office.

- In the absence of a statutory time limit on the length of detention and any independent review process for the ongoing decision to detain, legal safeguards are vital. The lack of access to quality legal advice and representation undermines the effectiveness of bail as a mechanism for safeguarding children who are detained. Families with children are often unable to access quality legal advice and representation at an early stage in the decision-making process. These problems are exacerbated in detention. The impacts of incompetent or unscrupulous legal advice and representation are particularly damaging for separated children whose age is disputed and who are often unable to access formal age assessment procedures.

- There are gaps in policy and practice for protecting children from abuse by adults when they are in detention. There is evidence that children may be returned to their country of origin without issues of possible abuse being resolved. There are particular issues about children whose age is disputed who are detained in communal sleeping facilities with adults and looked after by staff who have not been subject to enhanced CRB checks.

Recommendations

- Legal advice and representation should be available to all detainees. Financial thresholds should be reviewed to incorporate automatic additional time for representing detained clients. Access to bail should be actively facilitated and properly funded.

- A statutory time limit should be introduced when children are detained. This time limit should be a maximum of seven days. If, for whatever reason, removal cannot be effected during that time the family should be released from detention and alternative mechanisms re-established for maintaining contact and ensuring compliance.

- In the absence of a statutory time limit, there should be an independent process for reviewing all cases where children are detained. Such a review needs to take into account all aspects of the decision to detain, related not solely to the possible or anticipated immigration-related outcomes but the welfare outcomes for the child arising from his or her continuing detention.

- Welfare assessments should be undertaken for all children who are detained at seven and 21 days. These assessments should be made by an independent welfare panel, which should be established within each removal centre where families with children are held. The panel could also be responsible for reviewing the decision to detain and for ensuring that a family is released from detention without the requirements associated with the bail application process where there is evidence that children's welfare and well-being are being negatively affected.

- Children subject to immigration control should be recognised as children first and migrants second and their interests and needs represented by the Commissioners for Children and Young People in England, Wales, Scotland and Northern Ireland.

- All staff – and not just those coming into contact with children in families – should undergo enhanced CRB checks.

- Age-disputed individuals should not be detained unless and until there is a formal age assessment undertaken by social services or an independent panel. If age-disputed individuals are detained they should be held separately from adults and looked after by staff who are subject to enhanced CRB checks

- Children within families about whom there are child protection concerns should not be removed from the UK unless and until these issues are resolved.

Notes

50 House of Lords Hansard, April 27th 2004 Col 714, available at http://www.parliament.the-stationery-office.co.uk/pa/ld200304/ldhansrd/vo040427/text/40427-09.htm
It is not clear who Baroness Scotland is referring to when she comments on '99 other families'.

51 Article 5(2) of the ECHR requires that 'Everyone who is arrested shall be informed promptly, in a language which he understands, of the reasons for his arrest and of any charge against him'.

52 Home Office Press Release, Stat 054/2003, 16th December

2003, available at www.ind.homeoffice.gov.uk/ind/en/home/news/archive/2003/december/government_welcomes.html

53 Letter from Lord Bassam to Lord Avebury in response to written questions, dated 5th July 2004

54 Although most detainees at Oakington have access to the services of IAS and RLC, families detained as part of the Detention Overspill Facility (DOF) do not automatically get this access. If they make contact with these organisations, legal advice and representation are made available to them.

55 *Howard League for Penal Reform v SSHD and Department of Health* [2002] EWHC 2497

6 Conclusions

This report has set out the key findings of our research on the detention of children in the UK for the purpose of immigration control. These findings suggest that there is currently a substantial gap between the stated policy objective of detaining children only as a measure of last resort and for the shortest possible period of time and the reality of current practice. In light of this disparity, the research highlights a number of workable alternatives which illustrate clearly that the immigration detention of children can and should be phased out altogether.

6.1 The gap between policy and practice

It is clear from the evidence collected during the course of this research – and in particular from the experiences of children presented in this report – that detention can have serious impacts on the mental and physical health of children and that many of these consequences are long term. For separated children who are detained as adults and for whom none of the existing facilities are available, the impacts of detention are particularly damaging.

This report has suggested that despite contravening international standards set by the UNCRC and UNHCR, and despite evidence of the negative impacts of detention, increasing numbers of children are being detained in the UK for the purpose of maintaining the integrity of immigration control. Children are detained as part of fast track procedures for immigration even though the family's removal is not possible at the point where a decision is made to detain or as part of the process of removal when the Home Office considers a final decision to have been reached. The failure of enforcement staff to undertake a proper case review based on evidence about all the family's circumstances collected during a pastoral visit prior to a decision to detain, can result in the unnecessarily or prolonged detention of children where there are no imminent prospects for their removal. The absence of formal age assessment procedures for those whose age is disputed means that separated children can be detained, sometimes for lengthy periods and with no recognition of their needs as children.

There is currently a lack of alternatives to the immigration detention of children in the UK. Our approach to alternatives is based on the need to improve information and contact between the Home Office and asylum applicants in order to reduce the perceived need to detain families in order to speed up the processing of asylum claims or as part of the process for removing them from the UK. While reporting requirements provide one mechanism for achieving this objective, currently these are often inflexible to the needs of families and there are no incentives – in terms of information or support – to comply.

Our report has also identified a number of safeguards put in place by ministers in response to concerns about the impacts of detention on children and the effectiveness of existing processes. Many of these safeguards are designed to ensure that children are not detained for lengthy periods of time without a resolution to their situation and ensure that the UK detention practice is in line with domestic and international standards. In practice we have found such safeguards may be inaccessible – due to a lack of access to quality legal advice and representation – or meaningless, either because they are simply not undertaken in practice or because they are conducted internally within the Home Office and are based on incomplete information.

6.2 An entirely different approach

These findings lead us to conclude that there are four main issues that need to be addressed if the detention of children for the purpose of immigration control is to be avoided.

The first of these, and a recurring theme throughout the report, is the need for improved statistical information about the detention of children and greater transparency regarding procedures and processes. At a very minimum, statistics on the average length of detention and the number of ministerial authorisations granted and refused should be made publicly available. In addition, disaggregated data on absconding, removal and voluntary return would improve understanding of the context in which the decision to detain children is made and the policy rationale. If, as has been suggested by Government ministers and by Home Office officials with whom we spoke during the course of this research, the average period of detention is very low because the majority of families with children are removed from the UK within a few days of being detained, it would seem to be in the interests of transparency that this information is collated and published on a regular basis as part of the Home Office's quarterly statistics. The lack of information about the number of asylum-seekers whose age is disputed by the Home Office – both in general and specifically relating to detention – raises particular concerns because it is difficult to assess the scale of the problem and the risks to those who are potentially separated children.

The second key issue running through this report is the need for improved information provision and contact management. Loss of contact between the Home Office and asylum-seekers often leads to assumptions that a family or individual has absconded and is unwilling to comply with immigration controls, even though this may not in fact be the case. Moreover, it means that there is a lack of information about the asylum process as a whole or about the options for voluntary return when it is safe for families to return home. Our research has found that certain factors reduce the naturally low rate at which asylum-

seekers abscond, lose contact with the authorities, or fail to comply with directions for their removal. The provision of competent legal advice and concerned case management for example – which serves as a non-intrusive form of monitoring and which ensures that asylum-seekers fully comprehend the consequences of non-compliance – has been found to raise the rate of their appearance and compliance. Legal support, guardianship and specialised group homes run by non-governmental agencies have also been found successfully to reduce the rate at which separated asylum-seeking children disappear in several European countries. Available figures suggest that these alternatives are universally more cost-effective than detention. Our proposed alternative model for delivering contact and information – through the use of incentivised compliance initiatives with individual caseworkers and improved access to quality legal advice and representation from the beginning of the decision-making process – would improve the integrity and quality of the decision-making process as a whole and ensure that any decision to detain children is fully informed by all the circumstances of the case.

Allied to this issue is the need for better access to legal remedies throughout the decision-making process and in detention itself. In the absence of statutory time limits on detention, it is essential that internal administrative reviews of the decision to detain are effective and that there is access to legal safeguards including bail. Nowhere is this more necessary than in cases involving the detention of children. The evidence presented in this report raises significant concerns about the effectiveness of existing review procedures. In the absence of proper independent welfare assessments, this concern extends to the process of ministerial authorisation. None of these safeguards is available to children whose age is disputed.

Finally, and directly linked to this concern, the evidence presented in our report suggests the approach to cases where the Home Office disputes the age of the applicant needs to be entirely different from that which currently prevails. This approach assumes that these individuals might be adults claming to be children and that they should be treated as adults if the integrity of immigration controls is to be maintained. In the context of a growing body of evidence that many of these individuals are actually separated children, the risks of such an approach are extremely high. These children are vulnerable to abuse, the impacts of being detained may be particularly severe and they are at risk of being removed to their country of origin without full consideration of their application for asylum. For all of these reasons, it is vital that mechanisms are established for systematically dealing with age-disputed cases. This process should take priority over immigration control considerations. Once age is established, the case can be dealt with as appropriate. Until that time, however, consideration must be given to the fact that the individual concerned may actually be a separated child.

While there has been a considerable increase in efforts to ensure that children in the UK do not 'fall through the gaps' in provision and support intended to protect them from abuse, children who are subject to immigration control have been excluded from these measures. This is due largely to the assumed conflict of interests between the best interests of children and the integrity of UK immigration control. The alternatives to the immigration detention of children proposed in this report require an entirely different approach towards this group of children: one that places their needs and interests as children at the centre of decision-making. Our evidence suggests that this is not only in the best interests of children but will have positive implications for the quality and integrity of the asylum process more generally. To this extent, the conflict of interest between the best interests of children and the integrity of UK immigration controls – which is often cited as the justification for the current approach – does not necessarily exist.

If the Government is serious about protecting and safeguarding the interests of children in the UK, then asylum-seeking and other migrant children must be treated as children first and foremost and afforded the same rights and protection as other children. The failure to do so not only creates a culture where it is acceptable to treat some children differently (and worse) than others but – as the experiences presented in this report suggest – can and does have devastating consequences. It is in the interests of all children that the workable solutions we have proposed are listened to and taken forward, and that the immigration detention of children is made a thing of the past.

Summary of recommendations

Policy context

- The UK Government should review its practice in line with international standards and guidelines that state asylum-seeking children should not be detained.
- The UK Government should withdraw its Reservation to the UNCRC.
- Children should not be detained as part of fast track procedures for asylum determination.
- Detailed statistics on the immigration detention of children should be published on a regular basis. These statistics should include information on the overall numbers of children detained and the average length of detention. Statistics should also be published on the number of asylum applications involving age-dispute issues, including the numbers that are detained.

Impacts on children

- Because of the negative physical, mental and educational consequences of detention, children should not be detained for the purpose of immigration control. Alternatives should be developed for ensuring compliance where this is considered necessary.
- Further action needs be taken to monitor and significantly reduce transfers between different detention centres, particularly where these involve children.

Gaps between policy and practice

- The most effective way of ensuring that the decision to detain children is fully informed is to ensure that those with ultimate responsibility for

the decision to detain – enforcement officers working on the ground – are able to access the family's case file at first hand.
- A pastoral visit should be always be undertaken prior to a decision to detain. The aim of this visit should be to ensure that all the factors relevant to the decision to detain are taken into account. This visit should also be used as an opportunity to put in place alternative mechanisms for ensuring compliance which avoid the need to detain children.
- No decision to detain should be made unless and until a formal age assessment has been undertaken by social services. Better still, an independent age assessment dispute panel should be established comprised of independent social workers, experienced paediatricians and other relevant professionals. The establishment of the panel should be undertaken with the consensus and support of statutory and voluntary organisations in order to ensure that only one set of criteria is used for the process of age assessment in immigration cases. Age-disputed individuals should not be detained unless and until there is a formal age assessment undertaken by the panel.

Development of alternatives

- Case-by-case assessments should be carried out to establish whether it would be better for the child to be detained with his or her family, or separated. Parents and their children should be part of this decision-making process, in line with Article 12 of the UNCRC which gives children and young people rights to participate in decisions affecting their lives.
- Existing reporting mechanisms should be made more user-friendly and should be flexible to the needs of families with children. The Home Office should cover the financial costs of all reporting

requirements. Where reporting arrangements break down efforts should be made to re-establish contact before any decision is made to detain.

- The Home Office should pilot a system of incentivised compliance based on a reporting system that incorporates support, information, legal advice and representation and meaningful contact. This system should be based on the Appearance Assistance Program (AAP).

- Information about the opportunities for returning voluntarily to the country of origin needs to be made more widely available throughout the decision-making process in order that families are aware of all the options that are available to them if a negative decision is finally reached. Return under these circumstances must be truly voluntary in order for it to be effective and durable.

Safeguards for children in detention now

- Legal advice and representation should be available to all detainees. Financial thresholds should be reviewed to incorporate automatic additional time for representing detained clients. Access to bail should be actively facilitated and properly funded.

- A statutory time limit should be introduced when children are detained. This time limit should be a maximum of seven days. If, for whatever reason, removal cannot be effected during that time the family should be released from detention and alternative mechanisms re-established for maintaining contact and ensuring compliance

- In the absence of a statutory time limit, there should be an independent process for reviewing all cases where children are detained. Such a review needs to take into account all aspects of the decision to detain, related not solely to the possible or anticipated immigration-related outcomes but the welfare outcomes for the child arising from his or her continuing detention.

- Welfare assessments should be undertaken for all children who are detained at seven and 21 days. These assessments should be made by an independent welfare panel, which should be established within each removal centre where families with children are held. The panel could also be responsible for reviewing the decision to detain and for ensuring that a family is released from detention without the requirements associated with the bail application process where there is evidence that children's welfare and well-being is being negatively affected.

- Children subject to immigration control should be recognised as children first and migrants second and their interests and needs represented by the Commissioners for Children and Young People in England, Wales, Scotland and Northern Ireland.

- All staff – and not just those coming into contact with children in families – should undergo enhanced CRB checks.

- Age-disputed individuals should not be detained unless and until there is a formal age assessment undertaken by social services or an independent panel. If age-disputed individuals are detained they should be held separately from adults and looked after by staff who are subject to enhanced CRB checks.

- Children within families about whom there are child protection concerns should not be removed from the UK unless and until these issues are resolved.

References

Amnesty International (1996) *Cell Culture: The Detention and Imprisonment of Asylum-Seekers in the United Kingdom* London: Amnesty International

Amnesty International (2003) *Why am I Here? Children in Immigration Detention* New York: Amnesty International

Ashford, M (1993) *Detained Without Trial: A Survey of Immigration Act Detention* London: Joint Council for the Welfare of Immigrants (JCWI)

Australasian Society for Traumatic Stress Studies (2003) *Submission to the National Inquiry into Children in Immigration Detention*, available at www.hreoc.gov.au/human_rights/children_detention/submissions/astss.html

Australian Association for Infant Mental Health (2003) *Submission to the National Inquiry into Children in Immigration Detention*, available at www.hreoc.gov.au/human_rights/children_detention/submissions/infant.html

Ayote, W and Williamson, L (2001) *Separated Children in the UK: An Overview of the Current Situation* London: Refugee Council and Save the Children

Baldaccini, A (2004) *Providing Protection in the 21st Century: Refugee Rights at the Heart of UK Asylum Policy* London: Asylum Rights Campaign (ARC)

Barbed Wire Britain (2002) *Voices from Detention: Testimonies from Immigration Detainees in their Own Words*, available at www.barbedwirebritain.org.uk/voices.shtml

BID (undated) *Notebook on Bail (Parts 1 and 2)* London: BID, available at www.biduk.org/obtaining/notebook.htm

Blake, N and Drew, S (2001) *In the Matter of the United Kingdom Reservation to the UN Convention on the Rights of the Child* (legal opinion commissioned by Save the Children), available www.segregation.org.uk/legalopinion.pdf

Blake, N and Kilroy, C (2004) *Note on Implications in the Matter of R (on the application of A) v* SSHD, available at www.childrenslegalcentre.com/shared_asp_files/uploadedfiles/%7BB77EF00D-D6A8-470E-BFD7-AA9FCF2C6923%7D_Note%20on%20consent%20order%20_oakington_%2019.10.pdf

Bruegel, I and Natamba, E (2002) *Maintaining Contact: What Happens after Detained Asylum-seekers get Bail?* Social Science Research Paper, No 16 London: South Bank University

Chapman, N (1999) *Detention of Asylum-seekers in the UK: The Social Work Response'*, Social Work Monographs No 176 Norwich: University of East Anglia

ChilOut (2002) *The Heart of the Nation's Existence: A Review of Reports on the Treatment of Children in Australian Detention Centres*, available at www.chilout.org/files/ChilOut_report_to_DIMIA.doc

Cole, E (2003) *A Few Families Too Many: The Detention of Asylum-Seeking Families in the UK* London: BID, available at www.biduk.org/pdf/children/a_few_families_too_many_march_03.pdf

Cutler, S and Ceneda, S (2004) *'They Took Me Away': Women's Experiences of Immigration Detention in the UK* London: BID and the Refugee Women's Resource Project (RWRP), available at www.biduk.org/pdf/women/women_in_detention_in_word_%2002Sep04.doc

DfES (2003) *Every Child Matters* London: DfES, available at www.dfes.gov.uk/everychildmatters/pdfs/EveryChildMatters.pdf

DoH (2002) *Safeguarding Children: A Joint Inspectors Report on Arrangements to Safeguard Children* (October 2002), available at www.dh.gov.uk/assetRoot/04/06/08/33/04060833.pdf

ECRE (1997) *Research Paper on Alternatives to Detention: Practical Alternatives to the Administrative Detention of Asylum-seekers and Rejected Asylum-seekers* London: ECRE

Ehrenreich, R and Tucker, L (1997) *Slipping Through the Cracks: Unaccompanied Children Detained by the US Immigration and Naturalization Service* New York: Human Rights Watch

Fazel, M and Stein, A (2003) 'Mental health of refugee children: comparative study' *British Medical Journal* 327: 134, available at bmj.bmjjournals.com/cgi/content/full/327/7407/134

Field, O (forthcoming) *Study on Alternatives to Detention of Asylum-seekers and Refugees* Geneva: UNHCR

Hjern A, Angel B and Jeppson, O (1998) 'Political violence, family stress and mental health of refugee children in exile' *Scandinavian Journal of Social Medicine* 26: 18–25

HMIE (2003) *Update on Education Provision at Dungavel Immigration Removal Centre, South Lanarkshire* London: HMIE, available at www.homeoffice.gov.uk/docs2/dungavelupdate.pdf

HMIP (2002) *An Inspection of Dungavel Immigration Removal Centre* London: HMIP, available at www.homeoffice.gov.uk/docs2/ircdungavel03.pdf

HMIP (2004) *Report on an announced inspection of Oakington Immigration Reception Centre 21–25 June 2004* London: HMIP, available at www.homeoffice.gov.uk/docs3/ircoakington04.pdf

Home Affairs Committee (2003) *Asylum Removals: Fourth report of Session 2002–03, Volume 1: Report and Proceedings of the Committee* London: The Stationery Office, available at www.publications.parliament.uk/pa/cm200203/cmselect/cmhaff/654/65402.htm

Home Office (1998) *Fairer, Faster and Firmer: A Modern Approach to Immigration and Asylum*, London: Home office, available at www.archive.official-documents.co.uk/document/cm40/4018/4018.htm

Home Office (2001) *Secure Borders, Safe Haven* London: Home Office, available at www.official-documents.co.uk/document/cm53/5387/cm5387.pdf

Home Office (2002) *Voluntary Assisted Returns Programme: An Evaluation*, Home Office Research Papers No.175 London: Home Office, available at www.homeoffice.gov.uk/rds/pdfs2/r175.pdf

Hughes, J and Liebaut, F (eds) (1998) *Detention of Asylum-seekers in Europe: Analysis and Perspectives* The Hague: Kluwer Law International

Human Rights and Equal Opportunities Commission (2004) *A Last Resort? The Report of the National Inquiry into Children in Immigration Detention* Australia: HREOC, available at www.hreoc.gov.au/human_rights/children_detention_report/report/index.htm

Human Rights First (2002) *Country by Country Review of Detention Procedures and Practices* New York: Human Rights First, available at www.humanrightsfirst.org/refugees/reports/cntry_rev_02/country_reps.htm

Human Rights First (2004) *In Liberty's Shadow: US Detention of Asylum-seekers* New York: Human Rights First, available at www.humanrightsfirst.org/asylum/libertys_shadow/Libertys_Shadow.pdf

Human Rights Watch (1998) *Detained and Deprived of Rights: Children in the Custody of the US Immigration and Naturalization Service* New York:

ILPA and BID (2003) *Challenging Immigration Detention: A Best Practice Guide* London: ILPA and BID, available atwww.biduk.org/pdf/Best%20Practice%20Guide/bpg_challenging_detention.pdf

Ionel, D, McClean, N and Mobbs, A (2003) *Opening the Doors to Freedom* Oxford: Asylum Welcome

Joint Committee on Human Rights (2002) *Nationality, Immigration and Asylum Bill, Seventeenth Report of Session 2001–2*, House of Lords, House of Commons Joint Committee on Human Rights HL Paper No 132, available at www.publications.parliament.uk/pa/jt200102/jtselect/jtrights/132/13202.htm

Justice for Asylum-seekers Alliance (2002) *Alternative Approaches to Asylum-seekers: Reception and Transitional Processing System* Melbourne: JAS Alliance

McLeish, J, Cutler, S and Stancer, C (2002) *A Crying Shame: Pregnant Asylum-seekers and their Babies in Detention* London: Maternity Alliance, BID and London Detainee Support Group

Medical Foundation (2004) *Harm on Removal: Excessive Force against Failed Asylum Seekers*, London: Medical Foundation, available at www.torturecare.org.uk/publications/excforce.pdf

Mitchell, G (2001) 'Asylum-seekers in Sweden: An integrated approach to reception, detention, determination, integration and return', online paper available at www.fabian.org.au/library/event_papers_2001/1081751207_29216.html

Noll, G (1998) *Responding to the Arrival of Asylum-seekers: Unsuccessful Asylum-seekers – the Problem of Return*, Working Group on International Migration Working Group Paper No. IX/3 presented at the Technical Symposium on International Migration and Development, 29 June–3 July 1998, The Hague (unpublished)

Physicians for Human Rights (2003) *From Persecution to Prison: The Health Consequences of Detention for Asylum-seekers* Boston and New York, available at www.phrusa.org/campaigns/asylum_network/detention_execSummary/detention_pdf.pdf

Pistone, M (1999) 'Justice delayed is justice denied: a proposal for ending the unnecessary detention of asylum-seekers' *Harvard Human Rights Journal* 12: 197–265, available at www.law.harvard.edu/students/orgs/hrj/iss12/pistone.shtml

Pourgourides et al (1996) *A Second Exile: The Mental Health Implications of Detention of Asylum-seekers in the United Kingdom* Birmingham: Northern Birmingham Mental Health NHS Trust

Refugee Council (2003) *Children in Detention: A Refugee Council Policy Paper* London: Refugee Council

SCEP (2004) *Statement of Good Practice*, available at www.separated-children-europe-programme.org/separated_children/good_practice/index.html

Shackman, J (2002) *Criminal Treatment: The Imprisonment of Asylum-seekers* London: Prison Reform Trust

Silove, D (2001) 'Detention of asylum-seekers' *Lancet* 9266:1436-1437

Silove, D, McIntosh, P, Becker, R (1993) 'Risk of retraumatisation of asylum-seekers in Australia' *Australian and New Zealand Journal of Psychiatry* 27 (4): 606–12

Silove, D and Steel, Z (1998) *The Mental Health and Well-Being of On-Shore Asylum-seekers in Australia Psychiatry Research and Teaching Unit* University of New South Wales

Silove D, Steel Z and Waters, C (2000) 'Policies of deterrence and the mental health of asylum-seekers' *Journal of the American Medical Association* 284 (5): 604–11

Stanley, K (2001) *Cold Comfort: Young Separated Refugees in England* London: Save the Children

Steel, Z (2003) 'The politics of exclusion and denial: the mental health costs of Australia's refugee policy paper', unpublished paper presented at 38th Congress Royal Australian and New Zealand College of Psychiatrists Hobart, 12–15 May 2003

Steel, Z and Derrick, M (2001) 'The mental health implications of detaining asylum-seekers' *Medical Journal of Australia* 175: 596–599, available at www.mja.com.au/public/issues/175_12_171201/steel/steel.html

Stone, C (2000) 'Supervised release as an alternative to detention in removal proceedings: some promising results of a demonstration project' *Georgetown Immigration Law Journal* 14 (3): 673–687

Sullivan, E, Mottino, F, Khasu, A and O'Neil, M (2000) *Testing Community Supervision for the INS: An Evaluation of the Appearance Assistance Programme* New York: Vera Institute of Justice

Tarshish, S (1997) *The Care of Detained, Unaccompanied Children whose Age is Disputed* Oxford: AVID

Thomas, T and Lau, W (2002) *Psychological Well Being of Child and Adolescent Refugee and Asylum-seekers: Overview of Major Research Findings of the Past Ten Years*, Australia: HREOC, available at www.hreoc.gov.au/human_rights/children_detention/psy_review.html

UNHCR (1997) *Guidelines on Policies and Procedures in dealing with Unaccompanied Children Seeking Asylum*, Geneva: UNHCR

UNHCR (1999) *Revised Guidelines on Applicable Criteria and Standards Relating to the Detention of Asylum-seekers* Geneva: UNHCR, available at www.unhcr.ch/cgi-bin/texis/vtx/home/opendoc.pdf?tbl=PROTECTION&page=PROTECT&id=3bd036a74

UNHCR (April 2002) *Refugee Children*, Geneva: UNHCR, paper prepared for Global Consultations on International Protection available at www.unhcr.ch/cgi-bin/texis/vtx/home/opendoc.pdf?tbl=PROTECTION&page=PROTECT&id=3cd1544f4

Weber, L and Gelsthorpe, L (2000) *Deciding to Detain: How Decisions to Detain Asylum-seekers are made at Ports of Entry* Cambridge: Cambridge Institute of Criminology

Weber, L and Landman, T (2002) *Deciding to Detain: The Organizational Context for Decisions to Detain Asylum-seekers at UK Ports* Colchester: University of Essex Human Rights Centre

Wiesener, C and Corrigan, P (June 2004) *Measuring Misery. Detention of asylum-seekers in Northern Ireland: a statistical analysis 2002–4* Belfast: Refugee Action Group / Amnesty International, available at www.amnesty.org.uk/images/ul/M/Measuring_Misery.pdf

Zwi, K, Herzberg, B, Dossetor D and Field, J (2003) 'A child in detention: dilemmas faced by health professionals' *Medical Journal of Australia* 179: 319–322

Annex I Research interviews

Eric Avebury	House of Lords
Aamer Anwar	Beltrami Berlow Solicitors, Glasgow
Barry Bardwell-Snow	IRSS, Home Office
Simon Barrett	DPSU, IND
Keith Best	IAS
Syd Bolton	Medical Foundation for the Care of Victims of Torture
Eileen Bye	HMIP
Michael Connarty	Labour MP, Falkirk East
Sarah Cutler	BID
Judith Dennis	Refugee Council
Ian Duncan	Scottish Refugee Council
Susan Ellery	West Sussex Social Services
Jackie Gallop	MODCU, IND
Ophelia Fields	Research consultant
Nadine Finch	Barrister
Alison Hardie	IND (Oakington)
Penny Hart	IND
Alison Harvey	formerly at the Children's Society
Tina Heath	IRSS, Home Office
Helen Ireland	AVID
Helen Johnson	Refugee Council Children's Panel
Ailish King-Fisher	C&FPU, IND
Rachel Kirk	IRSS, Home Office
Amanda Little	Refugee Action
Ella Lyle	IND (Dungavel)
Steve MacCracken	C&FPU, IND
Kathleen Marshall	Children's Commissioner for Scotland
Adrian Matthews	Children's Legal Centre
Tom Narducci	NSPCC
Pascale Noel	Gatwick Detainees Welfare Group
Anne Owers	Her Majesty's Chief Inspector of Prisons
Brian Pinsent	RLC (Oakington)
James Purcell	IRSS, Home Office
Rajendra Rayan	RLC (Oakington)
Julia Recht	Scottish Refugee Council
David Rhys Jones	Medical Foundation for the Care of Victims of Torture
Astri Robinson	Department of Health
Jill Rutter	London Metropolitan University
Sally Tarshish	AVID
Clare Tudor	IAS (Glasgow)
Alison Venner-Jones	DfES
Mark Voce	IND

Annex 2 Roundtable participants

Simon Barrett	IND
Syd Bolton	Medical Foundation
Laura Brownlees	Save the Children
Sarah Cutler	BID
John Errington	Save the Children
Sue Fisher	Save the Children (Scotland)
Penny Hart	IND
Mohamed Jamil	IAS (Oakington)
Helen Johnson	Refugee Council Children's Panel
Miranda Kaunang	Save the Children
Sedi Keshavarzi	UNHCR
Richard Lumley	Refugee Council
Amanda McDowell	Save the Children
Richard Morran	Save the Children (Scotland)
Tom Narducci	NSPCC
Glevis Rondon	Children's Society
Susan Rowlands	ILPA
Jill Rutter	London Metropolitan University
Alison Venner Jones	DfES

Annex 3 Summary of case studies

Case study (CS)	Case type	Number of children detained	Age of child(ren)	Place of detention	Time detained (days)	Outcome
CS1	Family	1	13 months	Dungavel Tinsley House Oakington	61 in total	Removed
CS2	Family	1	0 months	Oakington Dungavel	161 in total	TA
CS3	Family	1	18 months	Dungavel	20	Removed
CS4	Family	1	9 months	Oakington	13	TA
CS5	Family	1	6 months (and mother pregnant)	Oakington	36	TA
CS6	Family	2	13 years and 10 years	Oakington	41	TA
CS7	Family	3	6 years, 4 years and 21 months	Oakington	48	'Probably' removed
CS8	Family	1	17 months	Dungavel	31	TA but later removed
CS9	Family	1	10 years	Dungavel	17	TA
CS10	Family	1	2 years	Tinsley House Oakington	3	57 (approx) Removed
CS11	Family	2	4 years and 9 months	Oakington Dungavel Tinsley house	162 (approx) in total	Removed
CS12	Age disputed	1	16 years when first detained, 17 when re-detained	Oakington Tinsley House	10	Bail
CS13	Family	2	7 years and 12 years	Dungavel	60	TA
CS14	Age disputed	1	16 years	Oakington	25	TA
CS15	Age disputed	1	16 years	Dungavel Oakington Harmondsworth	48 in total	TA

Case study (CS)	Case type	Number of children detained	Age of child(ren)	Place of detention	Time detained (days)	Outcome
CS16	Family	1	8 years	Oakington Dungavel	120 (mother only) 60	TA
CS17	Family	2	7 years and 5 years	Oakington	32	TA
CS18	Age disputed	1	16 years	Dungavel Oakington Tinsley House Harmondsworth Tinsley House	55 in total	TA
CS19	Age disputed	1	17 years	Police cell Tinsley House Harmondsworth	2 2 264	Bail
CS20	Age disputed	1	17 years	Oakington	18	TA
CS21	Age disputed	1	17 years	Oakington	7	TA
CS22	Age disputed	1	17 years	Oakington	7	TA
CS23	Family	1	5 weeks	Oakington	19	TA
CS24	Family	1	7 years	Harmondsworth Tinsley House Harmondsworth	7	TA
CS25	Family	2	18 months and 6 weeks	Oakington	Approx 26	Removed
CS26	Family	1	12 days	Oakington	43	TA
CS27	Family	1	2 years	Oakington	10	TA
CS28	Family	2	4 years and 20 months (approx)	Tinsley House Dungavel Tinsley House Oakington	2 separate periods of detention for 1 month and then 14 days	Removed
CS29	Family	1	5 months	Oakington	7	TA
CS30	Family	1	10 years	Oakington	27	TA
CS31	Family	2	7 years and 4 years	Oakington Dungavel	Children detained for one month with mother and father, mother continued to be detained	TA
CS32	Family	1	4 months	Oakington	116	TA

Total case studies = 32   Number of children detained = 41